Three More Days

Kate Morris

First edition 2024

Copyright © Kate Morris 2024

Cover Design by Sarah Duggan

The typewriter 'little bit of loveliness' is by Rhubarb Tree. Kay is a maker and crafter of beautiful things and has granted her kind permission for this image to be used. Visit www.rhubarb-tree.co.uk if you fancy a little treat.

All rights reserved. No portion of this book may be reproduced, copied, distributed or adapted in any way, with the exception of certain activities permitted by applicable copyright laws, such as brief quotations in the context of a review or academic work. For permission to publish, distribute or otherwise reproduce this work, please contact the author at kate@threemoredays.co.uk

ISBN: 9798332649875

Imprint: Independently published

A variety of fonts have been used throughout the book to differentiate the separate elements.

For Todd

An Explanation (also known as a prologue, I believe)

What follows is the story of the relationship between Todd and myself. It's a love story, a life story and a death story. A true story.

But why have I written it all down? It started when I was receiving counselling. It was suggested that I keep a diary in the weeks following his death. I was bottling a lot of things up and the counsellor thought it would help release a lot of my emotions. It did. It was hard to write (and to read again now), but it truly did help. Once I wrote things down, I seemed to break the loop in my head to some extent. Being a diary, I expressed my feelings fully. Everything was very raw and not necessarily logical. I have battled with some of the things I wrote, that were keenly felt at the time, but not as positive as I generally try to be. I decided to keep them in as I wanted this to be an honest account.

Sometime after Todd died, I realised I had no recollection of our history. I couldn't find any of our good memories. All I could recall were images of illness and death. It was terrifying. I was the only one left in the world who knew about us and I couldn't remember anything.

So, when those memories did start creeping slowly back a long time afterwards (at least 18 months later), I started to write them down. I couldn't risk losing them again. I grasped any little remembered thought or recalled moment and scribbled it into my notebook.

It seemed natural to add Todd's recipes into this. He had started a notebook with some of his favourite dishes in it, although sadly not his spectacular Beef Wellington recipe. Also, thankfully, not his dogfish curry! It was written in his dyslexic style and made me smile a lot as I tried to decipher some of the spellings. The quantities were wide-ranging too – sometimes catering for two, other times seemingly for about forty. But it was his voice. Please note that I haven't tested the recipes!

In the months after Todd's death, my job ended and I made the decision to move back to my mummy's, in Somerset. Most of our belongings went into storage and I returned to the bedroom I'd left at the age of 17. Before I moved back though I made the massive decision to travel to Australia for 3 months. My emails home are contained here too.

The medical facts of Todd's illness and death are also here, as by now it seemed I was writing a book whether I wanted to or not. I wanted this to be factual not emotional. I think it is all correct – it is hard to remember. I have used Todd's medical notes, his diary and my memory. I know more things happened but I don't know when. I know I have missed out all the stuff about Todd's night sweats which meant that the bedding had to be changed daily for example. And I know we had lots more visitors, but I'm relying on Todd's diary for those details and he didn't always note down who visited when he was really ill. I also know we got help from different people (like SAAFA) during this time too. But again, my memory isn't so good about all this detail.
It was a very hot summer in 2003. Todd was growing bamboo in our garden. It was going mad in the heat and growing fast. He kept a note of its height in his diary. Some normality in a world that had been turned upside down.

I chose the name, Three More Days, as after Todd died that is all I wanted. Three more days with My Boy. No visitors, no medical stuff, just us two. Three More Days…

Although I have obviously written from my perspective about my relationship with Todd, a lot of other people were, and still are, hugely affected by his illness and death. To help make sense of what follows, here's a sort of family breakdown. Anyone else mentioned is generally a friend of ours.

Jackie – Todd's Mum
John – Todd's Dad
Pat – John's 2nd wife, Todd's step-mother
Kim – Todd's brother
Penny – Kim's wife, Todd's sister-in-law
Sam and Harry – Kim and Penny's children, Todd's nephews
Nan and Gramps – Jackie and Mac's parents, Todd's grandparents
Mac – Jackie's brother, Todd's uncle
Ken – Jackie's 2nd husband (died 1993), Todd's step-father
Mark, Chris, Paul, Lisa – Ken's children, Todd's step-family
Lee and Julie – Todd's cousin and his partner
Scott and Rachel – Todd's cousin and his (then) wife
Helen and Paul – Pat's daughter and her husband
Elizabeth and Jennifer – Helen and Paul's children
Andrew and Alison – Pat's son and his wife

Anne – My Mummy
Tom (aka Thomas) – My Father
Sarah – My sister, my best friend
Kevin – My brother
Panda – Kevin's (now ex) wife, my sister-in-law
Rosie, Benjamin and Lilly – my nieces and nephew
Annie – Tom's ex-wife, my step-mother

The reason I wrote it all down? Because I want this to matter. I want Todd to matter.

Then

+

Before

Blue Sky, Green Grass

When asked for the umpteenth time,
"What are you thinking?"
Todd replied,
"Blue sky, green grass. What else should I be thinking?"

He was on his way to the hospital for yet another session of chemotherapy.

Blue sky, green grass.

Friday 30th May 2003

Having been sent home from work, Todd visits the Doctor's surgery complaining of diarrhoea, upper abdominal ache, pale stools, dark urine and loss of appetite. These symptoms have been coming on for the last 2 weeks. He is jaundiced. The doctor examines him and as Todd is a keen canoeist, who is often on the Thames, the doctor believes it may be Weil's disease or viral Hepatitis. He sends a referral on to the gastro-intestinal department and writes to the consultant. This department phones Todd the following week to offer an appointment – whilst he's lying in a bed on another ward.

JAUNDICE; yellowing of the skin and whites of the eyes, dark yellow urine, pale bowel motions and itchy skin. Jaundice can be caused by different illnesses including cancer of the pancreas. Jaundice can occur if the cancer develops in the head of the pancreas, and blocks the bile duct that carries bile from the liver to the intestine. The resulting build-up of bile in the body causes the symptoms mentioned above.

WEIL'S DISEASE; The disease is transmitted to humans by contact with the urine of rats, cattle, foxes, rodents and other wild animals, usually by contact with contaminated soil or water. The bacteria, enters the body via cuts to the skin, or via the nose, mouth or other mucous membranes. In most cases the infection causes a flu-like illness and severe headaches. The severe form of the disease causes jaundice and liver damage. Weil's disease is extremely rare. It is, however, a very serious illness, and must be swiftly diagnosed and treated.

VIRAL HEPATITIS; Hepatitis means 'liver inflammation'. Several kinds of hepatitis virus can infect the liver, but the most common are the hepatitis A and B viruses. Hepatitis A is caught through the contamination of food and water with faeces through poor personal hygiene or sanitation. (Or from kayaking in dirty water)

How it started

I met Todd on 13th February 1988. I was 17 at the time, doing my A levels. My friend Jackie had got me a job at the Oak House Hotel, in Axbridge, as a waitress. Todd was the Head Chef, he was 25.

I didn't like him to start with, he seemed very cross. He was a perfectionist with his food and he shouted if things weren't done his way. He was frightening! And he seemed to suck up to the customers. I now know it's called customer service. But when you are 17, that is not cool!

By April I had changed my mind. A couple of nights each week in his company made me realise what a good bloke he was. And he made me laugh. Cheesy jokes and throw-away chat-up lines filled the time when he wasn't shouting. He didn't stop shouting for many years.

One night we got locked in the walk-in fridge together. His team of chefs were jokers too. The door slammed shut and the light went out. Nothing happened. We laughed nervously and tried the catch. Nothing. We made some sexual grunting noises, playing along with the joke. But we weren't touching, just playing to the crowd. The door opened quickly as they tried to catch us out and we brazenly walked out, winking at each other.

Nothing had happened. Nothing and everything. I wanted him. A day later I left a postcard on his car windscreen with the message,
"See you in the fridge sometime"

Saturday 31st May 2003

Todd drives to Somerset and collects me from Mummy's house. We drive back to Oxfordshire and, in the evening, we go to the Oxford Playhouse to see Jo Brand. Todd is clearly in pain but doesn't want to leave early.

My Diary - Tuesday 1am

There are so many clichés in the world – it seems they are sometimes true.
It's true that you can be heartbroken. I felt mine snap when Todd went. And it hurt. More than I'd ever imagined it would. Actual physical pain that's all consuming.

And who knew how many types of tears there are? Tears that don't stop, whether you are awake or asleep. Tears that slide down your face silently regardless of where you are or what you are doing. Tears that are so violent that you think you'll be sick. Tears that make your whole body hurt. Uncontrollable tears rolling downwards. Silent tears. Silent screams. In the dark.

So much liquid from one person. Boots have made a fortune in tissue sales.

How can it be that I'm now visiting the doctor every three days to make a promise that I won't kill myself? How did that happen? I'm so lost without him. I can't bear to be without him. I don't know how to be without him.
I just want to be with him again. Just to hold his hand, stroke his neck, tell him that I love him again, hear that he loves me, again. We were always saying it – I love you – like a mantra. We meant it so much. That feeling is so deep within me.

I long for a glimpse of him. I hope that he will haunt me so at least I can still see him. Can he see me? Does he know how I feel? I was so strong for him during his illness. We said we would tackle it together. And we did. Together. Everything together. That's why I am so lost now. There is no together. Just falling apart.

When the light goes out at night I see him. Except, it's not the him I want to see – smiling, having a ciggie. It's him on his last day. Him suffering. Agitated and in pain. Telling me to

"Just go away" – his final words. It wasn't the romanticised vision I had in my head, where we told each other 'I love you' then did the right eye wink, left eye wink and blink thing. Our secret code. Not that. "Just go away". Body given up. Eyes not really seeing. Still trying to be independent. I just wanted to help. That's what I see when I shut my eyes at night. And I think I should have done more. Should have known what he was feeling. Should have known what to do to make it better. To take it all away. But I couldn't. I didn't know. So, instead, I beat myself up about it. Guilt is so deeply ingrained in who I am. And I feel it acutely now.

I feel guilty for his last day. I feel guilty that he got ill and I didn't. I feel guilty if I smile or laugh. I feel guilty if I don't think of him every moment of every day. And, mostly, I feel guilty because I am still here and he's not.

So, I try to hurt myself. External physical pain might block out the mental pain. Except I'm not very good at it. I've pinched and scratched. Dug in to create bruises but it doesn't help. And I'm too scared to do anything that will really hurt. My plan would be to take drugs to end it all. Enough to knock me out so that they couldn't bring me back. I'd do it on one of the days when there aren't any visitors. But there aren't many of those days at the moment. I'm being 'organised' – lots of visitors to keep my mind occupied. I know they mean well and I love them very much, but I just want to be left on my own. The grief won't come out unless I'm alone. I'm modifying my behaviour in front of guests. I feel there's a time limit on how long you can cry on someone's shoulder. So, I try to 'pull myself together' and mop up with yet another handful of tissues and make small talk. I think my Drama training is proving useful at the moment. I've always been able to put on a good show – now more than ever. 'She seems to be coping pretty well' and inside I'm planning to die. I don't want to carry on without him. He defined who I am.

I'd like a bamboo coffin, like his. I want to wear omething velvet, with lovely undies (matching obviously). But I don't want loads of make-up. I want star-gazer lilies, tulips, sunflowers, gerberas – they don't match. I have to think about it more.

I want 'Clair de Lune' for the committal music. Something by Pulp (F.E.E.LI.N.G. C.A.L.L.E.D L.O.V.E.?) and 'Summertime'. Oh, and 'Lovecats' by The Cure. Not sure how that all goes together. Seems a bit messy and chaotic. I need to think.

He wouldn't want me to do this. To plan this. He wants me to be happy. But that's just impossible. I'll only be happy if I'm with him.

But I'm scared that if I do it, go through with killing myself, then I won't be able to find him. Because I'd only be doing it so that we can be together again – for always. What if he wasn't there? He didn't believe that anything happened after death. No Heaven. No Hell. That was it. Full-stop. I don't know what I believe. I hope there is more than that because if there isn't I truly won't ever see him again, hold his hand, stroke his neck, tell him I love him and hear him say it to me. And that's unbearable.

Another break to my heart. My body is twitchy, my tears go unchecked – until I wipe my eyes because I can't see the page. I'm so tired but I can't sleep. I haven't slept properly since this all started. Not that that's a long time. It's still only just over 5 months since he first saw the doctor and I've been without him for 4 weeks. That seems surreal. It can't have been so quick. How could so much be fitted into such a short time?

Because its shit. That's how.

Tomato and Chilli Chutney

Ingredients
2lb Ripe Tomatoes
4 Cloves of Garlic
4oz Granulated Sugar
4oz Dark Brown Sugar
4oz Raisins
8fl oz Vinegar
2tsb Chilli Powder
1tsb Ginger Powder

Method

Blanche and peel the tomatoes. Cut in four and de-core.
Crush the garlic
Cook the tomatoes, garlic, ginger and chilli down to a pulp.
Add the sugar, vinegar and raisins and reduce until thick.
Allow to cool.
Store in clear, sterilised jars

An auspicious first date

After he'd worked out who the card was from (how many girls did he get locked in the fridge with?), a date was arranged. Thursday 21st April. I wore a flowery dress with a matching tie belt (sounds awful, but it was really pretty) and a little blue cardi. He wore grey trousers, grey patterned shirt and a red tie. The look needed some work, so did the choice of car — a silver Ford Capri, but there would be plenty of time for that.

I'd suggested that we went to the cinema in Wells to see Fatal Attraction. It was an 18 and that seemed appropriate as our relationship so far had relied heavily on sexual innuendo.

We arrived in Wells to find that Thursday night was Bingo night at the cinema. I was mortified. I realised at that young age that me and 'cool' didn't mix. Me and 'shambolic' was much more apt.

We ended up driving over the Mendips for miles listening to Pink Floyd and Phil Collins. I quickly learnt THE drum roll from 'In The Air Tonight'. It was played loudly and often, and audience participation was definitely required.

We arrived at a pub in Saltford, by the water. We sat in the garden and drank and talked. His taste in clothes may have been dubious, but so was mine in drinks — I was on Malibu at the time — ouch!

We told each other our life stories. Both had divorced parents. Both were the youngest child. But there were not many other similarities. We liked that, that we were so different. He drove me home. And phoned the next day and we arranged to meet again that night. No game-playing, fantastic.

***

I recently found the belt from that flowery dress when I was sorting out Todd's clothes. It was buried at the back of a drawer. The dress was thrown away years ago but he'd kept a memento. How many Brownie points does that deserve?

Sunday 1st June 2003

Todd is still in pain. I suggest he needs to go to A & E. He says he'll think about it, but insists that we go and do a big shop at Sainsbury's before he goes anywhere. When we get home, he agrees that A & E might be a good plan. I start phoning round to get a lift. Joe isn't home, but Lee is very willing to help. I pack an overnight bag for Todd, just in case. But I leave it in Lee's car whilst we wait in the department at the John Radcliffe Hospital. The last time we were here together, Todd had been abseiling down the maternity block – in aid of Cancer Research UK. Ironic?

Todd gets seen very quickly as he was given a doctor's note on Friday, in case something happened before his referral was actioned. Because he is so jaundiced, he attracts a lot of attention; it's a teaching hospital after all. We get lots of visits from student doctors, coming to see the yellow man. He is examined thoroughly more than once, including a rectal exam. No-one seems sure what the problem is. He is sent for x-rays but gets misdirected when he comes out and ends up in a queue along with the broken toes and wrists. This is a very long queue and his mood worsens. After unsuccessfully trying to get some help he rather vocally points out that he is in a large amount of pain, has had some bloke's finger up his arse and he is mightily fed up. As if by magic a nurse appears who takes his x-rays from him, takes one look and immediately whisks him back to a cubicle. As he is showing pain and tenderness in the upper right quadrant of his abdomen, but demonstrates no evidence of any mass he is referred to a general ward for further investigations. He needs the overnight bag. By now, Lee has gone home. I'm not sure how I got home – maybe I got the bus? I didn't drive back then. I know I had to start letting people know that Todd had been admitted to hospital, but that there wasn't anything to worry about. He'd be fine.

Monday 2nd, Tuesday 3rd and Wednesday 4th June 2003

Todd's diary reads; "First Day of the rest of my life!"

The first day back after half-term. Lots of chatter in the staff room about what they've all done with the week and then pretend horror at the prospect of being in front of their students. I was quieter than usual and this didn't go un-noticed by some members of staff. I told Lesley what had happened over the weekend and tried not to get upset, unsuccessfully. After briefing I was told to stay where I was. Someone else went and registered my tutor group. I was told that I needed to go to the hospital – to be with Todd. I was asked how I'd get there and, of course, said on the bus. 'Nonsense' was the response to this. If you can wait a little while the Caretaker will take you to Oxford. Bear in mind that this would be over a 40-mile round trip. So, Mike lived up to his job title and took me to the JR, it was very kind. I was told to take the time I needed.

I went to find Todd and the tests had begun. He had had loads of blood taken and been examined time and again. He went to have an abdominal ultrasound, along with all the pregnant ladies.

ULTRA-SOUND; This procedure involves exposing part of the body to high-frequency sound waves to produce pictures of the inside of the body. Because ultrasound images are captured in real-time, they can show the structure and movement of the body's internal organs, as well as blood flowing through blood vessels.

And he waited. He'd found where the smokers went – obviously – and would join them regularly. We spent lots of time in the canteen, sitting and talking about not a lot. He wasn't dressed like a patient. He didn't even own pyjamas at that point. He'd sleep in his underwear. They were lucky he'd do that. Normally he was naked in bed, as anyone who stayed at our house often found out...he frequently left the bedroom door open when he went to bed and subsequently threw the covers off himself. Such an exhibitionist! So, the only giveaway was the wrist tag which got checked incessantly. It seemed that no-one could even talk to him without checking his wrist details first – let alone carry out some procedure or other.

I spent the rest of the day with Todd in a sort of limbo. That carried on into the next day too. The ultrasound had shown an obstruction of the distal end of the bile duct which was 2.8cm in diameter. The gall bladder was also distended but there were no gallstones in evidence.

When I'd heard that they thought it might be gallstones, I thought I'd better return to work so on the Wednesday I turned up at school. Well, gallstones were nasty but not a reason for me to spend an extended time away from my teaching groups. The staff were surprised to see me and felt I should be back up in Oxford, until the diagnosis was certain. I was adamant I would teach and delivered 3 hours of Drama lessons before I had a non-contact period. However, the lack of noisy pupils in front of me gave me time to think and I realised that I ought to be with My Boy. I explained my change of mind and got on another bus. I went to M & S in Oxford and collected a BLT sandwich for Todd – he was not enjoying the hospital food. It was possibly the worst place that a chef could spend time!

I arrived to find John and Pat sitting with Todd. He was in a really snappy mood as I'd taken longer to get there than my text had said (it took 2 buses to get from Wantage to the hospital and often took in excess of 2 hours). I joked that maybe I should go home now, although I was somewhat pissed off by his greeting as I had come bearing gifts of things he liked to eat and more clean clothes, etc. The look on Pat's face said I shouldn't be joking and she and John left; to get a coffee, they said.

I asked how he was feeling and whether there was any news. And he told me. That's when the world stopped turning properly. He had cancer of the pancreas. Not only that but it had spread into the liver. It was terminal.

CANCER OF THE PANCREAS; This cancer affects about 7000 people in the UK each year, so it is not a common type of cancer. It most often affects people in middle and old age and is less common in younger people. The pancreas is part of the digestive system. It lies in the upper part of the abdomen, well above the navel, on a level with the V where the ribs meet at the front. It is deep inside the abdomen, lying just in front of the spine. It is about 6 inches long. The pancreas produces pancreatic juice (a fluid which helps to digest food) and insulin (a hormone which enables the body to use sugars and store fats).
Very little is known about the causes of pancreatic cancer.

SECONDARY CANCER OF THE LIVER; This is cancer that has started somewhere else in the body and has spread to the liver

He had had an ERCP on the 3rd June and it had shown an invasive tumour which was invading the duodenum and there was a large ulcer showing.

ERCP; This procedure allows the doctor to take an x-ray picture of the pancreatic duct and the bile duct using an endoscope. The bile duct can be unblocked during this procedure if necessary.

DUODENUM; The head of the pancreas lies next to the first part of the small intestine, which is called the duodenum.

Following this uncomfortable procedure, they had performed an urgent CT scan which confirmed the mass invading the duodenum. It appeared to extend into the pancreas and was compromising his common bile duct. When the scan was reviewed at the radiology conference it was felt that he also had liver metastases. The case was reviewed at the multi-disciplinary team meeting and the surgeons consulted. It was felt that stenting was the best way forward at this time.

CT SCAN; This is a series of x-rays which builds up a three-dimensional picture of the inside of the body. The scan is painless but takes longer than an ordinary x-ray. Special liquids are often used to allow particular areas of the body to be seen more clearly on the scan. They may be given as a drink or an injection, or both.

STENT; A stent is a short wire mesh tube that holds the bile duct open and helps to stop it getting blocked again. The insertion of a stent can relieve blockages within the bile duct and alleviate jaundice and other associated symptoms.

Gradually we found out more information. I would actively seek it out, I needed to know what to expect, whereas Todd was the opposite, so I kept what I found out inside. But at least I knew some things.

My diary - Thursday 11pm

Small steps. That's what I have to take. I don't feel I'm coping at all. Others seem to believe that I am. K2 said that I was doing well because I was out of bed, I was washed and dressed, the kitchen was clean and the lounge was tidy. How small can steps be? This week I've managed to go into town, alone. That's a really big deal. I didn't get too panicky, although I didn't make eye contact with anyone. Small steps.

I also got on a bus to Oxford and pretended that life was normal for a short time. I got very anxious when the bus home was late. Heart pounding.

Sweaty palms. Then I cried on the bus, but no-one noticed.

I had lunch with John and Pat yesterday. So much small talk. That's all we have. I can't believe the way they are acting about the money for the funeral. When I eventually brought it up, because they hadn't, they made me feel like crap. Like some money-grabbing gold-digger. I honestly thought that this wouldn't be an issue. It's the last thing they can do for him and they don't want to. They never have wanted to give him anything. When I think back, when the other children, his and hers, produced grandchildren, they were all given a bank account and a trip to Disneyland. What did Todd get? Fuck all! They are willing to pay for a trophy for the Canoe Club, but then that's visible generosity. I've always been so trusting of people's good nature – and even now I hope it will all come right, that the decent thing, the honourable thing will be done. But I have my doubts. This is the first time that I've been angry. It's not in my nature and I don't like it. And it all feels so unnecessary. I've got enough to deal with without crap about money. I wish I had enough to just pay it, but I don't. Pride can't even get me out of the inevitable sordid confrontation.

Then the sorrow starts to lap at my toes again, waves building up until I'm drowning again.

It never goes away. Sometimes I worry when I haven't cried for an hour because I'm going to forget. My throat is sore from keeping the sounds inside. Mummy's asleep in the spare room. I don't want to wake her. I have to get used to this. Get used to being alone. But I don't know how. I've always been with him. I moved from Mummy's house to his flat.

Wet face dripping onto the duvet. Every noise inside and outside the house is amplified. Every creak and rustle appears sinister. Childhood fears coming back to haunt me. I'm still not brave enough to confront those fears. I've always been a wimp. Todd was the brave and fearless one. He'd do it whilst I was thinking about it. Then he'd do it again whilst I was talking myself out of it.

I don't think I ever really told him how proud I was of him. I admired him. He was an amazing person. He touched so many people. So many at the funeral. So many back at the house.

I hope he liked what I did for him, I think he would. I tried my best.

Later

"Can I sit and read whilst you play on the water? I don't want to be soppy, I just want to be where you are"

Weekend of 7th & 8th June 2003

The stent was scheduled for the following week and Todd was allowed home for the weekend. I have no idea what we did.

I know that the Get Well Soon cards started to arrive, and so did the visitors. His mum, dad and step-mum had been to visit already. But that weekend, our friends started to come. And we'd tell them the news. I remember Todd asking certain friends around so he could tell them face to face rather than on the phone. It was very brave.

I'd been gradually letting people know Todd was in hospital but when the diagnosis came, I felt I had to make sure people were kept up to date. It would have been wrong to keep them in the dark. I didn't pass on the prognosis – there was no point at this stage. Only a very few people knew that.

My diary - 3rd May 2004

I'm on a plane on the way to Australia. How the hell has that happened? I no longer have a husband, a job or a home of my own but I do have a plane ticket and a cousin to stay with. And, surprisingly, a positive attitude.

I'd never have done this before. I'd have been too scared. But all the scary stuff has happened. This is just an adventure. I want lots of adventures now, I'm fed up of living for the future, living on dreams. Time to make some of them come true.

And now I'm at Singapore Airport waiting to re-join my flight to Oz. To me, it's 1.30 in the morning but here it's 8.30am. Very confusing. I haven't slept yet. I think I now need to hang on until I arrive in Sydney, 6.30pm their time. Bit of a walk on the beach, bit of supper, bit of a chat and a lot of bed I'm hoping!

Subject:	**sunburn? in the winter?!!**
Send:	**Mon, 10 May 2004 02:12:53 +0000**

hi everyone

well ive arrived! the flight was very very long with many films and a lot of food at odd hours. i only managed to sleep for about an hour during the whole time, but it didnt matter cos ive been sleeping so well since i got here...making up for about a year's worth of lost zzzzzz's!

i went down to bondi beach on my first night...we had a thai meal and then walked on the beach...wow! i went back a couple of days later to sit and look at the sea. it is a beautiful spot. and yes i got sunburnt! it didnt seem that hot. so now i have stupid tan lines as i was wearing a t-shirt and cropped trousers....duh!! everyone seems to think its very funny as it is meant to be winter here....winter? i'll show them winter! george and fay both went into work and told all their work colleagues about the burnt pom!

i went into sydney itself on friday and wandered by the opera house and watched the sun set behind the harbour bridge..cor blimey!

george and fay had a bbq on saturday....very australian! although no-one seemed to eat much. id done loads of salads and stuff, being used to foodie types and then realised i was with a crowd of beer monsters! it seemed the best way to proceed was to join in.....although i drew the line at 'straw-pedoes' (swallowing alcopops at great speed!) we played truth or dare jenga and i felt ancient!

on sunday i went to a football match.....!!!!! aussie rules stuff. im not sure what those rules were, but the little shorts and nice legs made up for it!! at the end everyone charged onto the pitch...and i thought...wahey its like a pitch invasion at home....but no, they were doing a 'kick to kick' where the crowd take on their own balls and have a kick about! bizarre!! i spent my time on the pitch ducking and cowering mostly!

today, im off to the zoo to see some koalas and kangaroos and stuff!

keep in touch...is great to hear from home...it seems a long way away

lots of love
kate
xxx

The sea, the stream, the sheep and the kiss

On the Sunday after that first date, we drove down to Porlock Weir. It was really quiet as it was still only April and the tourists weren't yet visiting. We walked along the pebbly beach, which was bloody hard work. Then we sat down by a tiny stream which was meandering its way down to the sea. It was making a gently tinkling noise, just audible over the sound of the surf. It's a good job I didn't need a wee!

We sat side by side on the rocks listening to the water. Our eyes met and we kissed, for a long time. All very Mills and Boon, but also very lovely.

We broke apart as we heard the rocks shifting directly behind us. Together we turned and saw a sheep watching us with a rather quizzical look on its face. Suddenly it was Mills and Boon meets James Herriott. The moment was gone. We walked back down the beach holding hands.

My diary - Friday 11.30pm

Tonight's thought – Curtains closing, David Grey singing "Sail Away", Jackie talking to Mac. Gentle sobbing.
And flames.
My darling boy's body being burnt. Being reduced to ash to be placed in an urn (bamboo, of course).

I don't know what to do with the ashes. I know I should scatter them somewhere significant. A favourite river maybe, or in the sea. Maybe Widemouth Bay. But I'm tempted to just bring him home with me. But then I'll never let him go – I'll turn into some mad old woman who talks to her dead husband's ashes. Do I care? I just want him back.

What did I do? What did we do to deserve this? Am I being punished for previous transgressions? I know I'm no angel, but who is? It's all so fucking unfair. But I couldn't choose anyone else to go through this. You wouldn't wish it on your worst enemy.

I know there are good memories in there. I just can't find them. So many good things to remember. But all I can see are vile images – some real, some imagined. Who invented such a hideously cruel disease? But I'd welcome it now – I think it's all I deserve. To feel his pain, to know that we will be together again. Forever.

Todd's 21st and Kate's 1st

May 1st 1988. A week and a half after our first date I planned a surprise for Todd. He had told me that his 21st birthday had been spent working in the kitchen at the Crumlin Road Prison in Belfast. As a chef in the Army, he had served all over the world. Belfast was not a high point in the early 80s. He was awarded a medal for the time he served there. Anyway, I digress. His 21st was not a good day. No celebration, just drinks in the squaddie's bar. As I was approaching 18, I thought this was awful. I knew I wanted to celebrate my big birthday and felt he should have done the same. So, when he collected me from home I had a box of goodies with me. When we reached his flat, I shut him in the bedroom and decorated the lounge with banners and streamers. I'd made him a birthday cake and even bought champagne. He was shocked.

After the cake was attacked and the champagne drunk (even though I didn't really like it) it changed from Todd's 21st to my 1st. First time that is. It just seemed right that Todd was the first man I slept with.

It was rubbish.

Spicy Buffet Sausages

Ingredients

1lb Chipolata Sausages
1/4pt Mango Chutney
1tsb Cayenne Pepper
1tsb Ground Ginger
2 Cloves Garlic

Method

Crush garlic.
Combine all ingredients and cover sausages.
Bake at 300F for 20-30 mins

All change

Things progressed very quickly between us. We were soon spending all our spare time together. Todd had his own flat so there was no need to be furtive with our love-making. Unless we wanted to be — the fear of discovery is always fun. We would spend our time going out for meals, visiting the cinema and at the flat.

We soon realised that we'd fallen for each other, that we were in love. Saying 'I love you' started very early in our relationship. Five months after the fridge, Todd asked me to move in and get engaged. We were lying naked on the lounge floor at the time — very romantic!

Before I would move in, I insisted on a few changes. I look back and think what a stroppy madam I was. I demanded that Todd redecorated the bathroom for starters, because I didn't like the dated 70s tiles. So, he took them down — and the walls came down too. The flat was full of surprises like that, nothing was ever easy there.

Getting rid of the Capri took somewhat longer but I did it. Now, I'd probably quite like having a silver Capri as I'm a big fan of retro and kitsch. But then I was just embarrassed. By lots of things.

Friday 13th June 2003

Todd had the stent put in successfully. Gradually his jaundice improved as his bile was able to drain away.

Subject: kate goes mad in the desert
Send: Mon, 17 May 2004 04:25:19 +0000

hi all

im writing to you all from alice springs this week. its in the middle of nowhere....the plane started descending yesterday and i couldnt see where on earth we were going to land! it truly is a remote place....but it still has mcdonalds and kfc!! ive been to the aboriginal centre this morning which was interesting. its very bizarre but alice is on the todd river. im near todd mall on todd street. ever get the feeling you are being looked out for?!

im off to ayers rock and the olgas tmw for 3 and a half days. its a camping trip. yes, you did read that right......im going camping!!!! ME!!

i had to hire a sleeping bag (im not even going to think how many people have used it b4!) as, surprisingly, i didnt have one! not sure how my mad jewelry and dalmation holdall will go down with the serious backpacker types!!

ive also booked to return to sydney on the train...its a very long journey and im stopping in adelaide on the way. i will be going on the ghan and the indian pacific (kevin are you jealous?!)

last week i did go to the zoo, which is in the most amazing setting. you have to get the ferry there across sydney harbour and its set on a hill so you can see the opera house behind the giraffes heads! i had my picture taken with a koala but wasnt allowed to touch. apparently you have to go to queensland to touch them. so i will be going there to get a hug.

i also went to the aquarium on a very rainy day. also an amazing place. another ferry trip to get there, eating fish and chips on the way. it doesnt get better than that! and i spent some more time on bondi beach, just chilling and doing some writing.

on saturday i went to paddington market...what a dangerous place that was....i spent far too much! and i know i will be going back. i'll just have to investigate how much it costs to send parcels back to the uk via surface mail!!!!

i got dropped at my hotel in alice yesterday and thought what a convenient location it was in....right by todd mall in the centre of town. however, when i went to check in i was told i was at the wrong aurora hotel. they called the shuttle back and now im staying in the middle of the outback! ho hum!! with a comedy bed.......that dips at the edges and the middle...quite special! better than camping though!!!!

looking forward to hearing from you all with your news and gossip...if you dont have any...make it up!!

lots of love

kate
xxxx

Arriving in Sydney after 24 hours travelling was a bizarre experience. I was greasy-haired and somewhat smelly. I was being met by my cousin George who I'd last seen at his sister's wedding. Luckily, I'd checked out his website to remind myself what he looked like. He'd not had that luxury and looked somewhat startled when a grubby, smelly blonde cousin approached him with a huge suitcase. He recovered quickly and ushered me into a taxi – no queues, no hassles. Not like Heathrow!

Within a few minutes, we were back at the flat and I realised why he was so shocked by my case. He and Fay lived on the top floor – up six flights of stairs. But being a total gentleman, he insisted on carrying it up without assistance.

Later that evening after showers and chats we walked down towards Bondi Beach and had a great meal at Thai Terrific, apparently their restaurant of choice when visitors arrived or left. We'd been to the bottle shop first as, like a lot of eating places in Australia, it was a BYO restaurant. A couple of Smirnoff Ices later I was feeling even more detached and confused than I had been earlier. We walked along Bondi Beach in the dark after the meal, listening to the surf – beginning the trend of permanently sand-filled trainers that would continue for my whole visit.

I collapsed into bed and surfaced about 15 hours later. I was alone in the flat as George and Fay were both at work. So, what did I do? I turned on the TV and watched daytime telly, Australia-style. I'd flown to the other side of the world on my own but now I was too scared to leave the flat in Bondi.

I was a mass of contradictions during my time away. I was sending home my very exciting emails (complete with excessive amounts of exclamation marks!), writing letters and postcards and phoning home too. In the UK I'm sure I looked as if I was having an amazing adventure. I was. But I was also experiencing lots of moments of crisis.

Along with the days following my arrival when I found it nigh on impossible to leave George and Fay's flat, I also experienced the same thing elsewhere.

For example, once I arrived at my hotel in Alice Springs I couldn't leave. I knew I wanted to go and explore but it took me over 2 hours to find the courage to go out. I was so scared of everything. I talked a good talk about not being frightened anymore…but I was. My heart would pound and I'd tell myself I didn't have to experience anything I didn't want to, to calm myself down. Yet, then I'd feel guilty as seemingly I'd travelled across the world to sit in a room. I could have done that at home.

It's true that you can't run away from your troubles, they follow you. Even 10000 miles to Australia.

But at least over there I had the element of control over the knowledge of my history. It was up to me who I chose to tell what had happened – or not. That was quite liberating. It was a stark contrast to where I'd been before – where I felt that everyone knew. Of course, that wasn't the case – paranoia and self-importance crept in there.

I was still taking the Prozac. It wasn't until much later in the trip that I started to wean myself off that. I dread to think what I'd have been like if I hadn't been on it at the beginning of my travels. Of course, I carried on being hugely emotional throughout the trip but I'm so glad that I went.

Even though I'd travelled across the world, a lot of my trip was comfortingly familiar. The language, the shops, driving on the left, the food – it all seemed close enough to what I knew. I think that's why I didn't choose to visit any other countries whilst I was away. I had the opportunity to break my journey in a selection of places but chose to just get there. I think anywhere too 'alien' would have been impossible for me.

Obviously, I did force myself out of my room in Alice Springs and went and explored and met Bill the Bus and then went on my first bus trip to the Red Centre. During that trip, I started to find my feet and became less scared. In fact, I was somewhat overwhelmed by it all. So much so that when I finished the trip and took the train to Adelaide, I felt compelled to write letters of thanks to the bus company and the driver guide. I later did the same to the guy who did my tattoos. It seemed important to thank people for making good things happen. And, of course, that is true – but I'd not done it before nor have I since. Maybe I should start again?

After three months I came back from Australia as my visa had expired. I could have stayed longer if I had travelled to another country and returned to Oz, but I chose not to. The day was the 5th August – it should have been our 9th wedding anniversary.

I've always celebrated anniversaries and birthdays as I feel it's very important to mark dates and celebrate the passage of time but coming back through all those time zones made our wedding anniversary spread into one hell of a long 24 hours – more like 36, I think! I was somewhat boggled by the end of it.

Moving out

Telling Mummy that I was moving out was one of the hardest things I'd ever done. We'd been living on a roller coaster together for years; her going through the menopause and me going through adolescence. We loved each other dearly but rowed incessantly. We'd always eat together but usually end up arguing at some point in the evening and I'd go off in a strop, slamming the door behind me. Like lots of households containing teenagers really — nothing unusual — just amplified because of the amount of hormones. I'd always been given tons of freedom from an early age. Kevin and Sarah had grown up and moved out and they had had all the tough rules. By the time it was my turn it seemed like a case of anything goes. She'd buy me and my mate Nicki cider to take to parties each weekend, and let me stay out late. But I wasn't much of a wild child.

Mummy and I were going to a farmhouse B & B in Aveton Gifford in Devon for a week's holiday. We went to the same place each year and shared a family room. Todd and I had decided that this would be the time to tell her that we were getting engaged and I was moving out. I was dreading it and kept putting it off. Each night I'd speak to

Todd on the payphone and have to say "I'll do it tomorrow", until the final night of the holiday. After my chat with Todd, I returned to the family room and told her.

She was so shocked. She refused to talk about it, just told me that I'd ruined the holiday. We returned to Somerset in silence the following day.

Soon after that I returned home one day to find that all the photos of me were face down. It was a horrible moment. Luckily my friend Jonathan was with me. I could tell he was as shocked as I was, but he tried to cheer me up. It didn't really work, but at least he could hold my hand. It seemed that I had been disowned. I felt I had to move out as soon as possible. I started to pack up my belongings. It didn't take long. And it all fitted in the back of the Capri.

I didn't want it to be like that. It was nearly my 18th birthday. This was all meant to be exciting. A new start for my adult life. Sarah was stuck in the middle of us both, trying to calm the situation down. But for weeks it got worse and worse. Until Mummy realised that if she didn't calm down, she'd lose me forever. She came round just before my birthday.

I had a party at the flat for my friends and Sarah came too. Todd got down on one knee at midnight, when it actually became my birthday, and proposed to me. Even at that moment we knew it was cheesy. But what the hell? We were never cool.

My actual birthday was spent at Mummy's. She had come around to the idea of us living together and being engaged. But what I hadn't realised was that she hadn't told Grannie. She had thought that it was just a whim and that it'd all blow over. Therefore, there was no need to tell Grannie as it would only upset her. Once she realised this wasn't the case, she told her. And Grannie promptly disowned me too.

Tuesday 17th June 2003

Todd discharged from John Radcliffe hospital.
Dental appointment 4pm
Weight 73.9kg
Oramorph 7ml @10.15pm

Wednesday 18th June 2003

Todd's diary notes his current drug list;
Metoclopramide 10mg (to relieve sickness) 1 taken 3 times daily
Creon 25,000 (assists with digestion) 1 taken 3 times daily
Creon 10,000 (as above) 1 taken with snacks
Lansoprazole 30mg (to neutralise acid and treat irritation in the stomach) 1 taken at breakfast
Lactulose 20ml (laxative) taken twice daily
Morphine Sulphate 80mg (pain relief delivered in a slow-release tablet) taken twice daily at 8am & 8pm
Oramorph 5-10ml (for breakthrough pain) as required
Ciproflaxacin 500mg (antibiotic treatment following surgery) twice daily until finished

Diary; Oramorph 7ml @ 5pm

Thursday 19th June 2003

GP visit. Dr Shackleton talks over the diagnosis with us both. We discuss Todd's pain medication. Morphine Sulphate morning and night, and Oramorph for breakthrough pain. She completes some forms for us and issues a month's sick note. Todd gives permission for her to talk to me about anything.
She later talks to Stuart from the palliative care team about his concerns over Todd's apparent lack of understanding of his prognosis. He feels that Todd believes he may still have years to live. Stuart knows that I am more aware of the reality of the situation.

Diary; Oramorph 7ml @ 6.15pm and 7.5ml @ 10.32 pm.
Kate's night off (slept well) (a night in the spare bed...supposedly to give me a good night's sleep)

Friday 20th June 2003

Diary; Mum visits
Oramorph 20ml @ 6-7pm

Saturday 21st June 2003

Diary; Upped Morphine Sulphate to 90mg 8am and 8pm
Kim, Penny, Sam and Harry visit in afternoon, Athene in evening.

Sunday 22nd June 2003

Diary; Dad, Pat and Helen visit, then Lee, Julie, Scott and Rachel, followed by Mary.
Oramorph 7.5ml @ 9.35pm

My diary - Sunday 1.45am

I dreamt about Todd last night. It's the first time. I don't normally remember dreams, but this one woke me up. It was the first time I'd seen him and how did I respond? I shouted at him! I got really cross. I can't even get it right in my dreams.

Mummy went home today. She obviously wanted to stay longer but I said no. Four days was enough. I feel so mean, but I don't want to be looking after anyone else for the time being. I know her hip is very painful and that she has an upset stomach – both very valid problems. But I begrudged the care I had to give her. And now I feel like a horrible bitch.

I held so much in whilst she was here. This time I felt like I couldn't cry again. Putting on a brave face and crying whenever I was in another room.

Since she left, I felt numb and then started crying at silly things. Everything seems to have an association, however tenuous. And when it doesn't, it's just as bad because I can't remember him through it.

I need to learn to drive so I can go back to our places alone. I know someone would always take me, but that's not the point. I need to go back and see if I can find him. He must be somewhere. He has to be.

My Heaven will have; the sea; cats; rabbits; guinea pigs; books; Beef Wellington; dark chocolate; crisp leaves; spring flowers; music; theatre. And Todd.

His would have; rivers; kayaks; the sea; cooking; singing; whistling; squash; running; cycling; roller coasters; juggling; egg yolks and animals.

So, I'll see him by the sea with some animals.

Like our first kiss, on the beach at Porlock Weir. Sitting on the pebbles with the little stream running down to the sea. Being interrupted by that sheep. Staring at us whilst we kissed.

Highbury Parade

Once I moved in to the flat, I had to change my A level courses. I had been taking English Literature, History and Economics (what was I thinking?) at my old school. I'd fought to get Theatre Studies onto the curriculum, but there weren't enough luvvies to make the course viable.

I decided to swap to the Sixth Form College in Weston and do my A levels there. But I didn't want to drop back a year, so I decided to do new courses in one year. I'd just do Theatre Studies and English Lit. Some of my friends were already studying there so I knew a few faces.

Mind you, I didn't take it very seriously which showed in my grades. I was having too much fun with my new life. I still wasn't wild at all, but I loved having our own space. I was playing at houses. In our free time, we'd go and visit places; have proper days out. We often went to places that had animals – Bristol Zoo, Cricket St Thomas, Tropiquaria, Monkey World and Longleat. Later on, we progressed to the Cotswold Wildlife Park and The Wellplace Zoo. We used to spend ages watching the animal's behaviour. We carried on doing that throughout our relationship going on dates to wildlife parks and zoos. I amassed a huge quantity of guide books. After Todd died, I had a plaque dedicated to him at Bristol Zoo's seal coast. "For My Boy". Enough said.

Todd gradually re-decorated the flat and the contents changed slowly. It stopped being a bachelor pad and became feminised. He even indulged my love of bears; stuffed teddy bears; ceramic bears; collectable bears.

There were shelves full of them. He even bought them for me. He must have really loved me!

I bought us new bedding and towels. It was the late 80s, so there was lots of floral, lots of cream and lots and lots of peach going on. I believe there may also have been 'Eternal Beau' crockery in evidence. The kitchen was grey and red. The lounge was magnolia. It was SO of its time.

When I moved in Todd had two fish tanks; one general fish tank which later moved into a particularly charming boxed-in area of the lounge – with false bricks surrounding it! The other tank housed Fred, the paranoid piranha. He was truly paranoid. He wouldn't eat if he thought someone was watching him. You'd have to stand on the other side of the room if you wanted to catch him snacking. Todd ended up selling Fred. And we got Bob instead. Bob was a black and white kitten, who somehow always seemed a bit feral. I think he may have left his mother too soon. He used to bite my knuckles as if he was trying to take milk. And his teeth were very sharp. As were his claws. He loved to climb; up doors; up curtains; up the ironing board (back in the days when I owned one); up onto the washing line (very disconcerting when you are lying in the bath, to look up and see a cat right above you); and me. Each morning as I was brushing my hair, he would climb up me and try to join in. it would have been funny if it didn't hurt so much. Bob moved out of the flat when I went to Devon the following year. Todd was looking after him at the time and one day he disappeared. We thought he might have been run over, but a few weeks later we spotted him living in a house on a nearby road. Cheeky bugger!

I loved our top-floor flat with the view over Steepholm. The sea could be seen from three of the four rooms (when the tide was in!). It was our own tiny home. There was an open fire in the lounge, Todd was always carrying buckets of coal up those stairs. There was a Calor Gas heater in the bedroom and that was about it for heating. Later we got a heater for the bathroom which made drying the washing a quicker activity. Before that, it used to take a week to dry, hanging on the clothes line over the bath.

The kitchen didn't have heating. That was Todd's domain. It was full of catering equipment. When I first moved in, he was still making and icing cakes as a bit of a sideline. Birthdays, Christenings, Anniversaries, Weddings, he did them all. He had loads of photos of his past cakes, and lots of cake-making and icing books too. The kitchen was full of cakes maturing, full of alcohol. There were icing bags and nozzles, containers of icing roses and other decorations, turntables, pallet knives and cake tins. He gradually stopped making cakes over the years. They were a very time-consuming sideline and he just lost the passion for it.

He did make our wedding cake though. A three-tier bear-covered extravaganza (we commissioned a local ceramicist to make the bears for us). Like I said he must have loved me, to indulge me in the bear theme so much.

During those months Todd had lost his job at the Oak House. The owner who had employed him had left and the new owners had their own chef so Todd was made redundant. The Oak House wasn't the same after he left. He looked for jobs for a while, trying out different Head Chef's positions before he ended up at the Arosfa Hotel in Weston and stayed for almost ten years. It wasn't like anything he'd done before, but he had a very strong work ethic so he got his head down and got on with it. In the past, he had worked at a range of expensive, well-considered hotels — working his way through the ranks. He'd done his initial chefs training in the Army Catering Corps. Like he said it was one of the best ways for a chef to train. His work had ranged from Officer's banquets to field catering to working in Northern Ireland. But despite the travel and people he met, he didn't want a career in the Services. So, he left and began his climb through the ranks in various hotels in the West Country. The Oak House had been his first Head Chef's job at the age of 24, not bad going. He was gutted when the job ended.

The Arosfa didn't focus on the same sort of cooking as at the Oak. It was much less fancy. Week after week there would be coach-loads of tourists wanting dinner, bed and breakfast. They would descend on the dining room en masse, wanting full breakfasts and a roast dinner in the evening. It was all nicely done and he always had other options available but mostly they liked their food traditional. These groups got to know him well, as they returned each year and he made the effort to make them happy. They did lots of functions there too, mostly Weddings but also Anniversaries, business meetings, etc. He was always manically busy but wasn't often stretched creatively. But he loved the fact that could walk to work in less than 10 minutes. And that walk took him along the beach, next to his big love — the water.

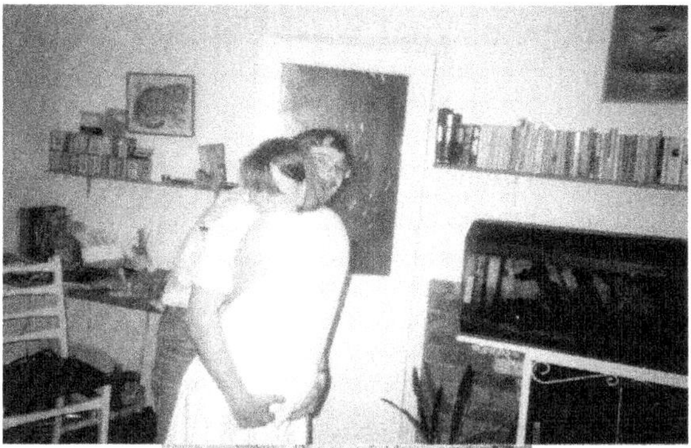

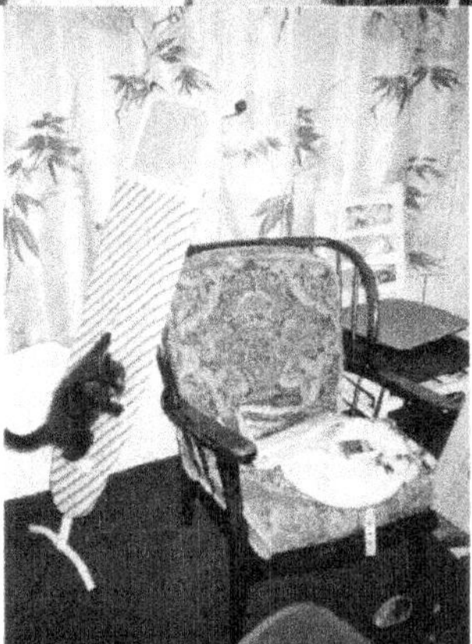

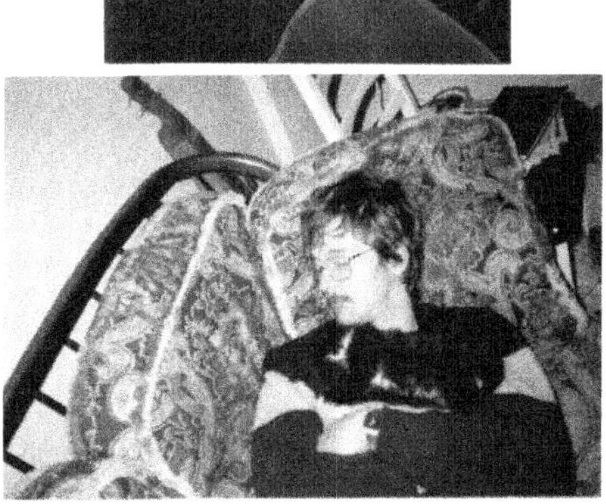

Escalope of Veal West Country Style

Ingredients

4x 8oz Veal Escalopes
8oz Cheddar Cheese Grated
1tbs Chopped Chives
1oz Butter
Salt and Pepper
½ Onion, finely chopped
1pt Cider
1pt Chicken Volute
1oz Butter
¼ pt Double Cream

Method

Lay flat the veal escalopes and lightly season.
Sprinkle over with Cheddar cheese and then the chives.
Roll up, as a Swiss roll.
Place a knob of butter on top and roll up in buttered tin foil, folding in the ends to seal.
Place in an oven at 350F for 20-30 mins
Meanwhile, sweat off the onion in the butter.
When soft, add the cider.
Reduce to 1/8 of a pint and then add the volute.
Simmer for 10 minutes.
Remove the veal from the oven and unwrap, adding any juices to the sauce.
Slice the veal ½ inch thick and lay on a warm plate.
Bring the sauce back to the boil, add the cream and lightly cover the veal.
Garnish with sliced apple.

Imago

After my, inevitably, disastrous A levels I found myself in a bit of a mess. Where now? I'd applied to and auditioned at Breton Hall in Yorkshire and Rose Bruford, nr London but hadn't been offered a place at either. I knew I wanted to pursue a performance-based future but couldn't see how.

Luckily my father, Thomas, spotted an advert in his local paper in North Devon looking for young people who wanted to spend a year working on Theatre in Education projects. It was unpaid but would be excellent experience. I would spend a year writing, devising and performing plays for schoolchildren and doing workshops with them too.

Our first play was 'The Selfish Giant' by Oscar Wilde, but re-imagined by us. I played the Sunshine and was a vision in yellow and orange. I did a lot of smiling.

Our other play was called 'Lechery Fair' and was based on songs and poems by Kurt Weill and Bertholt Brecht. It was designed for GCSE students. But after an open evening to show our work, all our GCSE customers phoned and cancelled. The play was considered too raunchy for their students. Looking back, I suppose it was a bit too much. It was all set in a cabaret and we were wearing underwear throughout. But the messages behind it were serious; it wasn't a piece of titillation. We quickly changed our target audience and performed to sixth-form students instead.

I made some good friends that year. I was very close to Becky as I lived with her, but Hermione's friendship continued. She later went to Central too and now acts and does a lot of voiceover work — it's odd hearing her as I watch TV. She was a rock when Todd was ill, and afterwards. He always used to fancy her like mad, so I was very pleased when she agreed to read at Todd's funeral. For his sake and mine.

That year was one of the best of my life. I was broke but doing what I loved — performing.

I went home every weekend to see Todd. I often worked at the Arosfa so I'd see him all day on the Saturday and then we'd spend Sunday together before he drove me back to Devon. Practically every weekend he trekked down to Beaford (I stayed with Thomas and Annie during the first term) and Barnstaple after that (when I moved in with

Becky and her family, sleeping on a mattress in her bedroom for six months. Mad!) He'd also made his bank account a joint account so I could have some cash each week. This was the beginning of a pattern of travelling home at weekends that would continue for about five and a half years.

During the year I auditioned for the Welsh College of Music and Drama in Cardiff and the Central School of Speech and Drama in London. I was ecstatic when they both gave me unconditional offers for the following year. I accepted Central straight away. Cardiff was closer but I thought London would be more exciting. And Central had a good reputation.

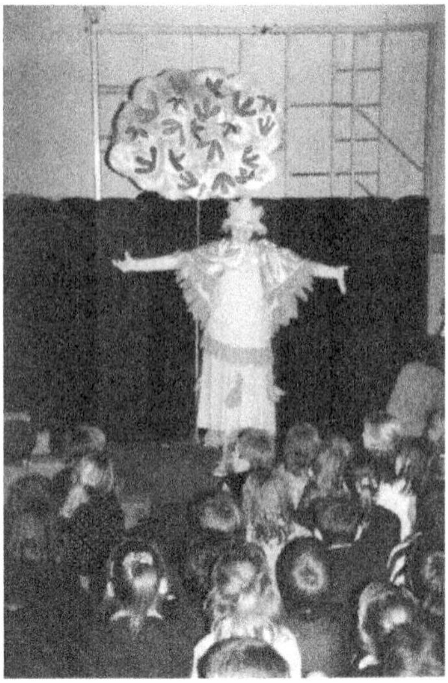

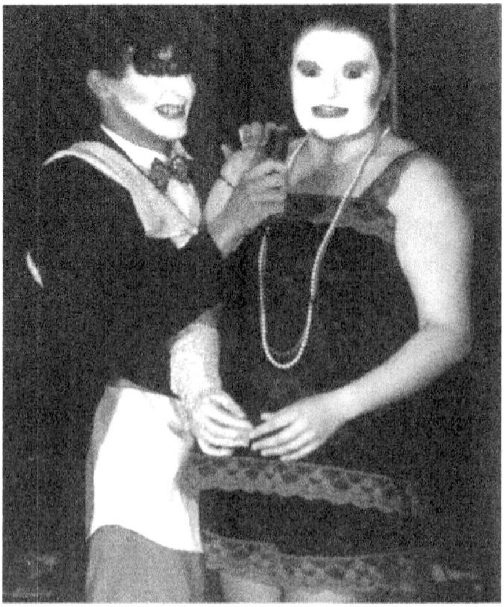

Monday 23rd June 2003

Diary; visits from Garry and then Kim
Bamboo measures 31"

Tuesday 24th June 2003

Todd gives consent for his employers to have access to his medical notes.
District Nurse visits.
Martin and Glenda visit.

Wednesday 25th June 2003

Dr Shackleton visits. We talk about my awareness of Todd's life expectancy. I am applying for Disability Living Allowance. Dr Shackleton takes her section of the form to complete.

DISABILITY LIVING ALLOWANCE (SPECIAL RULES); This fast-tracks the application and is for people with a life expectancy of less than six months.

Todd's Morphine increased as it was no longer controlling the pain. He is experiencing some nightmares with the Morphine but is OK during the day time.

Diary; Gas man working in the house.
Kim visits.
Kate's night off.

Thursday 26th June 2003

Diary; Pete and Ellie visit, followed by Kevin and then Vicki.
Oramorph 7.5ml @ 6.15pm and again @ 9.20pm

Friday 27th June 2003

Todd visits the oncology unit at the Churchill hospital in Oxford. He is currently suffering from pain, (although this is mostly contained with the Morphine), anorexia (weight loss) and tiredness. A range of tests are performed to assess his fitness for chemotherapy. He is given information about Gemcitabine and also for the Gem-Cap clinical study. He is asked to think about what he'd like to proceed with when he returns next week. He will need a further CT scan in order to fully stage him before treatment starts. He is told this is not a cure.

STAGING; The stage of a cancer is a term used to describe its size and whether it has spread beyond its original area of the body. Generally, there are four stages; small and localised (stage one); spread into surrounding structures (stages two and

three); or spread into other parts of the body (stage four). If the cancer has spread to distant parts of the body this is known as secondary cancer (or metastatic cancer).

Diary; 70.1kg
Upped Morphine Sulphate to 220mg.
Visit work and see colleagues.
Bamboo 34.5"
Sarah visits
Oramorph 7.5ml @ 6am
10ml @2.20pm
20ml @6.30pm

Saturday 28th June 2003

Diary; Bamboo 35.25"
Sarah staying
Kim, Sam and Harry visit
Oramorph 20ml @ 7.40pm

Sunday 29th June 2003

Diary; Sarah staying
Mum visits followed by Dad, then Tom Wood
Bamboo 36"
Oramorph 20ml @ 11am

My diary - Tuesday midday

I slept well last night. It was the first time for a long time. I've been avoiding taking the pills because I don't like them. But it had got to the stage where I had to. Maybe two or three proper night's sleep with the pills will help a bit.

I feel a bit calmer today. Or is that just numbness?

I don't want to go out today. I don't have to, I have enough fresh food for the animals to last until tomorrow. If I didn't have to get that I'd be able to stay in the house for ages without going out. The freezers are full, there's plenty of soft drinks and loads of rice and pasta (the benefits of living with a chef)

I love him so much. I can't bear that I'll never see him again, never hear his voice, never feel his touch.

I was sitting in the bath earlier and started crying because I couldn't call out to Todd to scrub my back. I let the water drain away but couldn't be bothered to get out. I stayed there for ages, getting colder and even more numb.

I can't be bothered to do anything much. An air of lethargy has descended on me. Except, it's far too heavy to be air.

Right Eye Wink

Somewhere along the way we developed a secret code between us. I was rubbish at winking and Todd would wind me up about it. He'd try to teach me to do it. I could manage the right eye OK, but the left was useless.

So, we'd go through this routine of right eye wink (success), left eye wink (OK for him, failure for me, cue giggling) and a really big vehement blink (which I was very good at)

It was one of those something and nothing actions that couples have, that no-one else notices, nor cares about. But it made us smile.

I always thought that would be our final communication. That whoever went first — and obviously, they would be very old at the time — would lie on their death bed, make eye contact with the other and go through the wink, wink, blink routine. Reality isn't often like dreams though.

Right eye wink, left eye wink, blink!

Subject: wow!

Send: Sun, 23 May 2004 04:21:53 +0000

g'day!

im in adelaide now...ive just arrived on the train from alice springs. the journey took 19 hours! and i have another 24 hour train journey to get back to sydney...boy, this country is big!!

i have just had the most amazing few days. i told you i was in alice springs last week...i forgot to mention 'bill the bus' who was driving the hotel shuttle bus. he recommended a few places to visit and then picked me up later. he then took me to see a group of rock wallabies being hand fed and then we went and watched the sun set from anzac hill....it was very kind of him, and i certainly wouldnt have done those things without some local knowledge.

on tuesday i set out for my trip to uluru, kata tjuta and kings canyon with some trepidation. there were 22 people on the tour, a really mixed bunch. it took about 5/6 hours to get near the rock and we missed the sunset on the first evening as the bus and trailer got caught in the sand. we had to push it out! v funny! then we loaded up with firewood and set off for the camp site. once we were there i headed for the kitchen (!!) and started preparing stuff...i didnt want to have to set up the tents to be honest! we had a very odd meal but it was fine...then we sat by the fire. i was persuaded to sleep in a swag (a sort of outside sleeping bag) under the stars. it was beautiful. but very cold..the next night i managed to use my winning smile to get another sleeping bag from the driver guide and then it was fine!

we were up at 5.30am to see the sun rise over ayers rock. then we drove closer and some people climbed it and some did the base walk. i did the latter as it seemed wrong to walk on it as it is a sacred site...you wouldnt walk over someone's church roof, so why climb over the rock? (plus it looked really hard!) then we had a BBQ and visited the aboriginal cultural centre. then back for another walk at the base...led by our guide...it was amazing...especially a waterhole at the end. a really peaceful spot.

then we watched the sun setting over the rock...there were lots of people doing that, with champagne and canapes (not us!)

the next day started at 5am, watching the sun rise over the rock again from another spot. then we drove to the olgas (kata tjuta) and went for a walk there...and guess what? give up? i put my knee out half way round!!! i had to be helped back to the bus by the driver, les. it was a very slow walk...poor bloke! but we got there...and before the rest of the group got back too which was a relief! then i wore an ice pack for the rest of the day and took painkillers! grrrrr!! everyone was great though, they really looked after me. it was an odd sensation, sitting round the camp fire with intense heat burning my shins and an ice pack melting on my knee!
by the next day, it was a lot better but i still only did the creek walk at kings canyon to be safe. that was another truly beautiful place. only 2 of us did the creek walk so it was very quiet. all i could hear was rustling branches, tinkling water and bird song...lovely!

then we drove back to our camp site for lunch and a camel ride!! hehe...very odd sensation!

then we started the drive back to alice, stopping on the way to see a performing dingo...possibly the most bizarre thing ever!

when we got back to alice we watched one last sunset from anzac hill and decided to spend the evening together as well. so we had supper at toddy's (!!) and went out to bojangles bar and drank rather a lot! i did dance quite a bit...my knee protested yesterday!

then onto the train yesterday afternoon. i was sitting next to one of the japanese girls who had been on my tour...another bizarre coincidence!

anyways, im off to explore. i'll write again in a few days.

lots of love
kate
xxx

ps. you know i dont 'do' backpacking?! well, ive given in...im staying in a
hostel in adelaide!

Central

I spent four years studying at the Central School of Speech and Drama in London. Each weekend I came home to Todd, sometimes on the train, but mostly on the Bakers coach, with Norma as our hostess, "Remember only number ones in the loo everyone. Thanking you kindly"

And each weekend I worked at the Arosfa alongside Todd. Drama student, in London, during the week and waitress in Weston-super-Mare at the weekend. With a fiancée who had saved up all of his dirty dishes for the week and left them festering in the kitchen. Welcome home Kate!

It wasn't always like that, but mostly it was. Sometimes I'd get in a strop about it, but mostly I tried to ignore it. What was the point in wasting our precious time together seething over the dishes? That's the problem with living apart — the expectation is that the time spent together will be somehow idyllic. It's not the case. Reality steps in pretty quickly, especially when you live apart for a lot of years.

I'd come home, decide whether to do the dishes or not (the main contributing factor to a positive decision to don the Marigolds was whether there was mould growing on the crockery!) But I'd always do the washing. I'd have to pre-treat nearly all of Todd's clothes. I wasn't even washing his whites then, he just spilt a lot! Watching TV and eating on your knee not being a great combo. Todd was exempt from using the washing machine by now. He'd had one too many washing disasters! And I'm sure he thought he had a Kitchen Porter at home as well as at work. He was a messy chef. I loved his food, but I didn't enjoy being his KP!

It wasn't always completely domesticated. We'd sometimes go away for the weekend. One time I took him away with money I'd saved from my Arosfa wages. It was a total secret. The destination, everything. Except I hadn't actually done it properly. When we got to Brighton, our secret destination, the B&B I'd booked looked awful so we had to find somewhere else. Somewhere cheap. I ended up finding us a place that wasn't much better than the original B&B. It had one of those beds that rolls you together. We spent the night clutching the edges so we didn't suffocate one another in the middle. Luckily it made us laugh rather than moan. We asked a local for a recommendation for somewhere to eat and were directed to something like a Brewers Fayre pub, "It's lovely there", he said, "you could have a steak if you wanted. With chips or a jacket potato. You can have sauce. Anything you want"

It sounded delightful, but not quite what we were after. We found a lovely restaurant and had a very expensive meal. It was one of those places that only has the prices on one set of menus…the person who is paying gets to see the cost. They immediately gave it to Todd, so I swapped them over quickly. I then realised that my idea of treating Todd for the whole weekend might not be possible, unless we ate McDonalds for the rest of the time! He paid for the second evening — when we actually went back to the same restaurant again.

He liked to surprise me too. He took me away for a secret weekend on the Isle of Wight. It was lovely. It was slightly out of season but not cold. We had a B&B right by the sea. We were able to walk back from dinner along the beach. And we could hear the surf from our bedroom window. Very romantic.

But mostly the Central years were filled with dirty dishes and waitressing. I'd spend my week learning to be a Drama teacher, going out on teaching practice at various schools in London, being involved in performances, learning about language and how to use your voice. I lived in Honor Oak Park, Wembley and Swiss Cottage. Mostly I shared with the same 3 girls from my course; Karen, Abs and Tracey. We got on well together; we must have done to live together for three and a half years. It wasn't perfect and we didn't always agree, but it seemed to work OK. We used to spend every Wednesday evening eating sponge pudding and custard and watching The Golden

Girls. Each of us became one of the characters. I was Dorothy...the very droll one with the deep voice. Tracey was my mother, Sophia. Karen was Rose, the ditsy one and Abs was Blanche, the slapper! The three girls later became my bridesmaids. I made some incredible friendships during those years, some of which continued, Karen, Carol and Garry especially. Our house, in Swiss Cottage, was often a venue for parties. It would fill up with students from all the courses and would be pretty mad. I was still Mrs Sensible though so I dressed in a somewhat Laura Ashley style — not really fitting in with the cool actor-ypes. I once got told that I looked like Janis Joplin at one of the parties. I had a tray of oven chips in my hand at the time and a floral frock on. I didn't really see the connection, nor was I particularly flattered.

Todd didn't often come up to London. He really disliked it up there. But he came up often enough for everyone on my course to know him well. And, of course, I was young and in love, so I never stopped talking about him. So, for four years I lived this odd halfy halfy life of London and Drama combined with Weston and Todd. It worked for us.

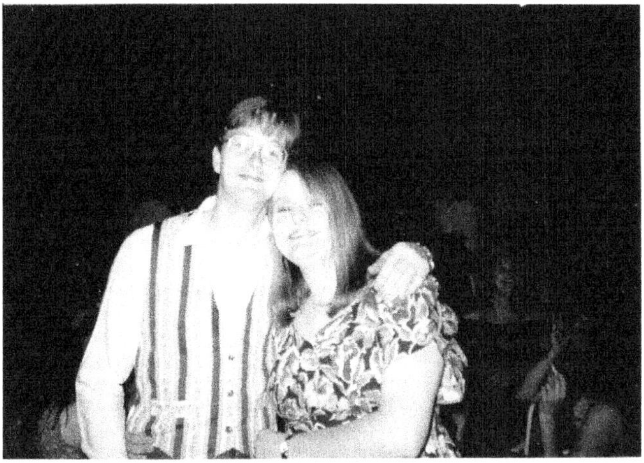

Monday 30th June 2003

Diary; Call Dr Middleton (oncology) before 10.45am
District Nurse visits
Oramorph 20ml @ 11am
10ml @ 7.15pm

Tuesday 1st July 2003

Diary; Bamboo 37"
KCC (Kingfisher Canoe Club) barbeque
Oramorph 10ml @ 1pm

Wednesday 2nd July 2003

See Dr Shackleton. Patient's condition worsened so has increased MST (Morphine Sulphate) to 140bd. Using Oramorph. Full torso CT scan this pm as part of chemo trial due to start Friday. Pruritus at night - menthol and aqueous cream, cool bedding and Piriton at night are suggested. Constipation and wind in evidence, burping and Rennie help. Increase Senna, Lactulose pm. Alter drugs slightly.

CT scan at Churchill hospital 3.45pm

PRURITUS; excessive itching

Thursday 3rd July 2003

Diary; Wok at Work day at IHS – goes ahead without Todd
Oramorph 20ml @ 8am

Friday 4th July 2003

Chemotherapy starts. As well as the standard chemo, Todd begins the Gem-Cap trial too. It's a mixture of intraveneous drugs delivered over a couple of hours in the chemo suite and tablets to take at home – 3 weeks on, 1 week off (like the Pill!). At least he doesn't have to wear an ice-cap. Doctors increasing constipation drugs. Chemo tends to create diarrhoea so this should balance it all out.

CHEMOTHERAPY; this is the use of anti-cancer (cytotoxic) drugs to destroy cancer cells. There are many different chemotherapy drugs. Some are given on their own, but some may be combined. Chemotherapy is given for different reasons; to cure cancer; to reduce the chance of cancer returning; or to shrink a cancer, reduce symptoms and prolong life. This is known as palliative chemotherapy.

ICE CAP; Ice caps sometimes retard hair loss from chemotherapy

Diary; Sarah arrives
MST increased to 160mg
Weight 67.45kg

Saturday 5th July 2003

Diary; Sarah staying
Bamboo 38.5"
Pain in shoulder
Oramorph 20ml @ 10pm

Sunday 6th July 2003

Mark (Ken's son) and family visit. First time they've seen each other in years. Bit stilted and emotional but OK. Promises made to keep in touch but feel it's unlikely.

My diary - Wednesday 12.30am

I went out with Lesley tonight. We went to the theatre, in Oxford, to see 'Fosse' which was good. I had to get the bus there which was OK. I was fine with Lesley. We talked about her pregnancy and school, anything but the big stuff.

It was all fine until I got home and realised that the house would be empty. Nothing would have moved or changed since I left. How ever many lights I'd left on, it didn't make any difference. I was still going home to an empty house.

It's not so bad in the daytime, because he wouldn't have ordinarily been there so the empty house feels like it's waiting for his home time.

At night though – it's where he should be.

I know this sounds like nonsense. But then my life doesn't make sense, so why should this page?

And Then I Got High

Todd liked to get high. A lot! He'd been trying to get me stoned for a long time. But because I didn't smoke it proved a bit of a problem. I'd tried smoking his spliffs but I just choked and got red in the face. I never got anything from it. He started devising recipes – foods to make you smile.

He started with cakes that he'd cook in the microwave. They were vile! All you could taste was the blow and you had to eat half a cake to get any effect. It was like a punishment rather than a pleasure.

Then he hit upon hash fudge. It took a lot of tweaking to get the recipe right but eventually he did it. It had a high proportion of Cadbury's Dairy Milk in it to mask the taste of the resin. It didn't take much to get you smiling.

Its popularity spread and he'd make it for my friends and his. I even got given an award at the end of Central – "The Mrs Beeton Award For Services To Confectionery" My boy, the stoner!

Mix and Match Recipe For The Fudge That Will Blow Your Mind

Ingredients

4 lb Granulated Sugar
1 pint Whipping Cream
¼ pint Milk
250g Butter

Method

Put all the ingredients in a thick bottomed sauce pan and heat to hard ball on a sugar thermometer.
Melt 800g CDM.
Pass 1 oz of cannabis resin through a sieve and when the sugar mix is ready, pour over the cannabis and whisk for 5 mins.
Add the chocolate and whisk for a further 5 mins.
Pour in to tins and chill for 4 hours.
Enjoy.

Makes 18 x 6 oz
20 x 5.5 oz

Mix & Match Recipe for
The Fudge That Will Blow
your mind.

4 LB Granulated Sugar.
1 PT Whipping Cream.
¼ PT Milk
250 G. Butter.

Put All Engreadance in a Thick Botomed Sauce Pan and Heat To Hard Ball on a Sugar Thromiter

Melt 800 G of C.D.M.

Pass 1 oz of Conibos Resin Though a Sive and when The Sugar Mix is Ready Pore over The Conibos and Whisk it for 5. Mins. Add The chocolate and Whisk for a further 5 mins. Pore in To Tins and chill for 4 H

Makes 18 × 6 oz   ENJOY.
        20 × 5.5 oz.

Monday 7th July 2003

Diary; Nurse visits
Kim visits

Tuesday 8th July 2003

The company who run Todd's workplace write to Dr Shackleton, requesting information about Todd's condition and his prognosis.
I take my Driving Theory Test (on Todd's insistence) and fail.
Diary; Joe visits, followed by Lee and Keira. Bamboo 39"

Wednesday 9th July 2003

Kevin visits, followed by Dad and Pat.
Dr Shackleton visits. Patient's condition the same. Has increased MST to 160bd. Pain mostly controlled but referred shooting pains in right shoulder – not better with MST. Constant irritation with severe exacerbation for ½ - 1 hour daily, usually at about 7pm. Eased by lying down. Advice given. Try Amitriptyline 1-2 at lunchtime. May need to vary time and dose to ease later pain.
Appetite improved.
Fatigued. Significant change since chemo started 5 days ago – sleeping lots.
Pruritus improved, less at night with Pirition and Aqueous and menthol. Works well when needed.

Constipation improved. Better since Glycerin suppositories. Constipation related pain gone now. Advised to increase laxatives as analgesia increases.

Thursday 10th July 2003

Nurse takes blood test prior to next chemo session.
Lee visits, followed by Chris.
Bamboo 39.5"

Friday 11th July 2003

Diary; Chemo (phone prior to leaving house to check it will go ahead)
Kim takes us to the hospital

Sunday 13th July 2003

Panda visits and does reflexology on Todd's feet.

My diary - Thursday 11pm

'It's all right. You can come out now. Wherever you are. I'm sorry for whatever I've done. I'm so sorry Todd. It must be really bad to be punishing me like this'

I seem to be 'coping' and 'moving on'. To an outside eye that's how it seems. I fool myself sometimes.

My insides still feel like they are ruptured though.

Numb then tears.
Numb then tears.

I'm trying to have a night without a sleeping pill. I was very tired when I came upstairs. But as soon as I enter the bedroom, I'm wide awake again. Haunted by images that I don't want to see.

'Just go away'

Is It A Bird?

Todd loved being active. He was an incredibly fit man, despite all the fags he smoked. He played squash, ran, cycled and kayaked. But he went through a stage when we lived in Weston where he loved roller-skating. Not blading, but proper skates. He would travel up and down the seafront all the time. He was also a keen juggler and often would juggle and skate at the same time. He loved to entertain people. We both did. I'm sure he is part of the reason that they put up 'no skating' signs on the seafront in Weston. He was quite distracting with his juggling balls, rings and clubs.

I gave him a present of a weekend at the Circus Space in London one birthday. He loved it and couldn't stop talking about it and practising his new techniques, which now included plate spinning and Diablo. His enthusiasm was amazing. He'd totally throw himself into new interests with a huge passion. He was like a big kid.

He even juggled small children sometimes. He'd make them shriek with delight as they got thrown from one arm to the other, whilst he kept the juggling balls in the air at the same time.

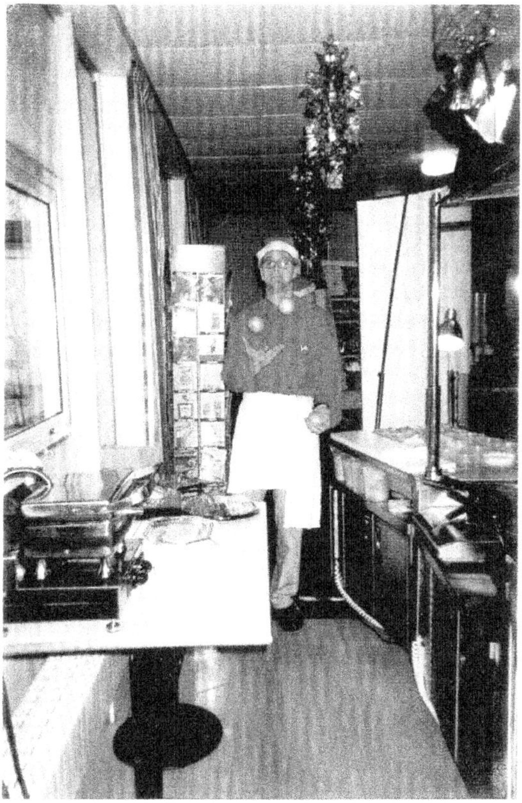

Subject: just a thought
Send: Thu, 27 May 2004 04:26:49 +0000

just a quickie today.

im back from adelaide, but a bit boggled....24 hours on an uncomfy train!!

so i will write more in a couple of days.

i was wondering if anyone wanted my snail mail address...its great to get emails...but real post would be even better! if u r interested it is....

kate morris
ocean street
bondi
sydney
nsw 2026
australia

maybe some english postcards to remind me of home?!!! the cheesier the better.....prize for the winner!!

lots of love
kate
xxx

A Hoe Of A Time

My first teaching job was in Plymouth. I thought it would be lovely. In Devon, near the sea. A new laid-back life. Todd had plans to open a deli — it was all perfect. It was even a beautiful day when I went for interview. I should have heard alarm bells ringing when I got advised how to break up a fight during one of the one-to-one sessions. Those bells should have been clanging when I never saw a pupil or the inside of a working classroom, despite being there all day. And I should have trusted my gut instincts and said 'no' when I was offered the job. But I didn't, I accepted. It was my first proper job interview and I didn't want to get blacklisted for mucking a school around. There were all sorts of horror stories circulating Central about blacklisting.

Then I cried all the way back to London on the train. I thought after I calmed down that it would be OK, it wasn't though. I was miserable there and ended up resigning and leaving at Christmas, having done one term at the school. It was an awful start to my teaching career and would have a massive effect on my future.
At Christmas, I went back to Weston. But this time I didn't leave again. Eventually we were living together all the time

after five and a half years of weekends and holidays. It took a bit of getting used to. But it was good, we were planning our wedding for that summer. And now I would be nearby for all the arranging.

I found work as a supply teacher at two schools in Weston. I did most of my work at Priory, where I had done my final teaching practice. Supply teaching wasn't lovely; in Science I ended up with test tube clips attached to my jumper; in another classroom, some kids had an aerosol can and a lighter and we had a flash fire under one of the desks; and in Games, I never knew the rules so I had to get one of the students to run the lesson. But it paid the bills.

Monday 14th July 2003

Dr Shackleton returns medical report to St Andrew's group. It states that Todd is too unwell to continue his occupation at present and may not be able to resume work at all. She gives an overview of his symptoms and confirms that his condition falls within their definitions of a malignant tumour and is not one of the specifically excluded types. She encourages them to expedite any payments in view of the serious nature of the disease.
Diary; Mum visits, followed by Bridget.

District Nurse calls by.
Bamboo 40"

Tuesday 15th July 2003

Diary; Kate (Macmillan Nurse) due to visit but cancels
Hermione visits, followed by Paul.

Wednesday 16th July 2003

Dr Shackleton notes that patient's condition improved. Generally, better in himself. More energy. Pain well controlled – has not needed Oramorph for some days and no increase in MST. Shoulder pain gone since using Amitriptyline 10mg at lunchtime. Off to Bude on hols next week. Going to try Oramorph unit dose vials. Advised to try cutting back on MST – 10mg every few days.
Sick note completed for 6 weeks.
Constipation improved, normal bowels on Lactulose and Senna. Gripey abdominal pains also gone now.
Nausea symptoms worsened. Past couple of days has vomited in mornings. But largely OK for rest of day. Advice given about swapping anti-sickness drugs. Prescription given in case.

Thursday 17th July 2003

Pre-chemo blood test taken

Sunday 20th July 2003

Todd admitted to Ward 6F at the John Radcliffe hospital. Small bowel obstruction secondary to tumour. Gastrointestinal meal shows duodenal invasion/encasement with significant hold up in stomach. During this admission has been able to tolerate oral intake, but will need a surgical bypass.
Doctor's notes; in hospital for a significant duodenal obstruction. Gastrojejunostomy planned for 28.7

GASTROJEJUNOSTOMY; Surgery carried out to treat a blockage in the duodenum, if the blockage is causing vomiting. During the operation, a piece of the small bowel (the jejunum) is connected to the stomach, to bypass the duodenum

Chemo cancelled
Diary; 67kg
Bamboo 40"
Hermione visits, and then takes us to the hospital.

My diary - Friday morning

'Please come back to me.

I tried so hard to protect you from it all, but I failed in the end, didn't I?

I just want you back so much'

Later

'I need you to look after me. You always protected me, made me feel safe. And now I don't feel safe at all. Just scared. And exposed.

Why was it so quick? It's so fucking unfair. We should have still have been going away together, spending time together alone. What time we did have was filled with people. I worked it out, after your diagnosis, we only had 3 days alone together before you died. 3 days with no family, friends or medical people. 3 days in Cornwall. Just us.

And now they have all slotted back into their lives – same surroundings, same people in bed next to them at night. And I'm left alone. Begging for 3 more days and then 3 more and then 3 more. I'd give up anyone else if I could have you back. I'd sit alone in a room with you for eternity rather than go through this.

I've made your pillow wet with my tears again. I'm sorry.

I'm remembering that time in Bude and feeling guilty again. Guilty for pushing you too much. Guilty for not having a drink to hand when you needed it. Guilty for forgetting your sunglasses. And I know I shouldn't. That should be a good time to remember. You wouldn't want me to remember it sadly. But, as I said before, I can't seem to find the good memories. I'm so lost and so frightened.'

Sunshine Radio

During my time supply teaching in Weston, I saw a feature in the local paper, the Weston Mercury, about the hospital radio station. They were looking for more volunteers. I put myself forward as it seemed a good thing to do for the community and, less altruistically, I could improve my microphone skills! I started on Ward Round. You would visit a ward, collecting requests and chatting to the patients, then return to the studio, find the music and then introduce it on air. I developed a fine knowledge of some shockingly bad music. It was all very middle of the road but appealed to my kitsch side.

As time passed, I got trained to operate all the studio equipment and moved from just being a guest Ward Rounder who introduced pieces of music, "for Joe on Cheddar Ward, here's Perry Como. Get well soon Joe" to having my own show.

Monday's Nightflight became my own. I'd be on air from 9pm til 10.30pm each week. I'd play lots of cheesy music, do a quiz (no-one ever entered), read a Joyce Grenville or Victoria Wood monologue and witter away for an hour and a half, safe in the knowledge that no-one was really listening. They were merely awaiting the time when we flipped back to Radio 2 for the night.

Todd used to arrive sometime after the 10 o'clock news to pick me up and I'd play '3 in a row' — slushy songs that I'd dedicate to him. He'd make fingers down the throat gestures as I tried to remain sincere. '3 in a row' always gave an opportunity for a bit of a snogging. Although, you did run the risk of getting caught out by anyone wandering the corridors late at night, who could see straight into the studio.

Again, I met some lovely people (people mostly are I think) — Astra, Robbie, Gemma and Andy all came to our wedding.

During my time there I sent a promo tape to some local radio stations. I had meetings at two stations. Galaxy FM, in Bristol, told me that they loved my voice, found the tape amusing and that I should go away and get some more experience. I did it. I had my own hospital radio show. But did I pursue that lead? Nope. Another missed opportunity. Kate being a scaredy-cat. Again.

Subject: lots of travel and lots of sneezing
Send: Sun, 30 May 2004 08:54:57 +0000

hello everyone

a quieter week this week. i really enjoyed exploring adelaide...a really attractive city, with beautiful old architecture set against massive skyscrapers. i found the contemporary craft galleries...of course i did!! my purchases didnt really fit in with the hostel atmosphere! on my second day there i caught the tram down to the sea at glenelg. it was lovely. i wandered round then lay on some grass by the sea and listened to the tide coming in. smile time!

then on the following day i caught the indian pacific train from adelaide to sydney. my advice to anyone considering the journey.......dont!!! or if you do, get a sleeper berth! somehow it was worse than the ghan...less spacious and definitely in need of some tlc. anyhow, the time passed (all 24 hours of it)...obviously! and now im back in sydney.

but, boo hiss, i have a crappy cold and cough...i sound v pathetic when i cough....but my voice is very husky!! that'll be because it is 'winter' here you know!! ive been trying to ignore it all and carry on with the good stuff. i went to 'the rocks' this afternoon. its an area by the harbour bridge. there was an art event on there this weekend, with artists painting all along the quay...v cool! there were also stalls to see and street theatre to watch. i watched one guy for about an hour....he was british and pretty good. as i was waiting to put a few bucks in his collection, someone asked him where he was from.....he said street in somerset!!!

talking of theatre..i went last night. i saw a play called 'backpacker' at the darlinghurst theatre. it was ok....bit wooden in parts but fun! it was a really nice little performing space....made me want to leap up and start performing myself!! (garry, do u fancy being a techie again?!!) mind you its odd going to the theatre alone.,.much easier to go to the cinema.

thats something i have done a bit, in adelaide especially. i saw 'eternal sunshine of the spotless mind' there (v good...jim carrey didnt do any rubber-faced stuff!) and 'the company' (beautiful dancing...just no story!). on the trains they play films too....so ive also seen 'almost famous', 'school of rock' and 'whale rider' over the last few days. its the sydney film festival over the next few weeks so i can keep up my square-eyed hobby!

i have the flat to myself until 14th june as george and fay have gone back to the uk. its very nice to have some space and time to myself. im not used to being so sociable!

anyway, like i said, a quiet week, so i shall stop waffling now!

keep in touch

lots of love kate
xxx

Roller Coasters

Todd was an adrenalin junkie – I clearly wasn't. I'd talk myself out of doing anything the tiniest bit frightening, yet he'd be at the front of the queue.

Hence our different choices for our Stag and Hen parties. Neither of us wanted the bar/club experience (with the obligatory 'L' plates and veil for me and the getting stripped and padlocked to a lamp-post for him!). I chose to go to The Comedy Store in London and then on for a meal with my bridesmaids and some other girlfriends. And Todd went to Alton Towers for a day of white knuckles and screaming – well, I'd have been screaming. He wouldn't be cos he was a 'bloke' and blokes aren't meant to scream, are they?!

He went on The Big One in Blackpool years later. In the photo that gets taken half way around he had totally white knuckles and his skin was pulled back but he loved it. He came off buzzing. Can't understand it myself!

Knowing how much he loved that adrenalin rush, I bought My Boy a bungee jump for his 40th birthday. He didn't actually do it until the following Spring when he combined it with an abseil down the John Radcliffe hospital building in Oxford. Bungee on Saturday. Abseil on Sunday. He raised loads of money for Cancer Research. Like I said previously, dramatic irony there somewhere.

Wednesday 23rd July 2003

Discharged from JR to be re-admitted on 28/7 for triple bypass on 29/7.
Chris visits.

Thursday 24th July 2003

Diary; Gen and Kate visit.
Kate visits counsellor for the first time.

Friday 25th July 2003

Doctor writes letter to Financial Assurance.
Diary; Thea visits.

Saturday 26th July 2003

Due to go to Bude, to join Kim and family on holiday for a few days. Cancelled.

Sunday 27th July 2003

Diary; Dad and Pat visit.

My diary - Saturday midnight

What's the point? I feel like I'm running on autopilot.

Sarah was meant to be coming down today and staying the night, but she couldn't come as her legs are bad again. I feel selfish because I needed her visit this weekend. I know she isn't well, who is at the moment? And I try to be sympathetic, like I do with Mummy, but it feels as if my caring reserve has run dry.

Mind you, if I'm looking after someone, at least I have a purpose in life.

It took me hours to get the courage to go out of the house. I hadn't been out since I came back from the counsellor on Thursday morning. I only went out because the animals needed more food and I needed to know what was on the TV. It blocks out the silence. Todd needed the noise it provided when he was ill. Now I need it because he has gone.

I kept my head down, trying to avoid eye contact. I bumped into a girl from my tutor group. She was really pleased to see me and then I could see her getting embarrassed, not knowing what to say. Then I saw a sixth former, who was very sweet. She asked if I was going back to school. I just don't know. The thought of it is terrifying. I don't want a deadline because that just gets more threatening. They seem to think I'll be going back next term. I don't know if Martin has told them that or what, but I haven't mentioned dates to anyone. It seems very close. And I don't feel nearly ready. That would be acting, the biggest performance of my life. "Character of Drama Teacher Coping Surprisingly Well After Tragic Loss"

Last night I tried a night without a pill – but I ended up taking one at 1.30am because I wasn't tired. Well, I was, but my body wouldn't let me sleep. The intention was to try without tonight, but I'm much more awake than I was when I came to bed. I have to be careful as I don't have enough to last me until the next doctor's appointment on Thursday.

The Wedding Of The Year

5th August 1995

Todd had proposed to me way back in 1988, it seemed like this day would never come. We'd decided that we would get married the year after I graduated as I would have had a chance to earn some money by then. Obviously, this hadn't gone quite according to plan but with a little monetary help from our families we would manage.

I'd been planning the day for so long. I had years-worth of bridal magazines dotted around the flat. Becky and I used to spend hours designing my dress during the Imago year. At that point my dress had a medieval feel to it. She'd even designed one of those pointy hats with a piece of chiffon attached to the tip. Good job we didn't get married then as I probably would have gone through with the design.

But we waited.

It was a real family affair. Everyone got involved. Kevin played the organ in the church. Todd's mum, Jackie, made my dress and the boys' waistcoats. Panda, made the little bridesmaids dresses and B's waistcoat. Annie decorated the church with flowers, my cousin, Amanda, got the raw silk for my dress, Tom went to France with us to buy the wine, Sarah decorated the hall, Todd did the main cooking and the cake and Sarah, Mummy and I prepared salads. It was a mad time. Everyone got very involved.

There was no need for wedding cars as I walked with my 'procession' to the church past the graveyard. Along the path that I used to dash down when I was on my way to the bus stop to go to school, or shopping in Weston. The path I used to take when I was on my way to work at the Oak House. Kevin had been sent out during the morning to clear the path of dog crap — poor bloke!

The wedding was during one of the hottest summers we'd seen for ages. The grass was parched and brown in the pictures. There were so many photos. The photographer, Mac, a family friend, was very thorough. But it took ages and was so hot that people got a bit bored...and started on the booze!

It was a lovely ceremony. My friend Carol read a poem, my niece, Rosie, surprised us by playing the violin during the signing of the register. I had Sarah, my nieces and nephew and Karen, Abs and Tracey as my bridesmaids and page boy. OTT? Maybe a little!

Todd had his brother, Kim, as his best man and Gen and Wayne as ushers. Tom gave me away.

It was all pretty traditional and the vicar even asked the congregation to pray for children for us. That was an unlikely wish for us as we were decidedly anti-children. They didn't register in our plans at all. We liked having nieces and nephews, but had no desire to produce our own small people. Not at that point anyway.

As we had done the catering ourselves and even got the wine from France, it meant we could invite lots of people. There were lots of family and friends and then more arrived in the evening. Although, as it was so hot, people kept disappearing into the Square to get some air.

I don't remember the speeches very well. To be honest, I don't remember big chunks of the day. I wish I had made a speech myself but I lost my nerve. Crazy. A performer who didn't want to perform. But I'd have been playing myself. The hardest role of all.

Todd got extraordinarily drunk and I found it very hard to separate him from Kim at the end of the evening. He was declaring, "you're my brother and I love you" through the streets until I managed to steer him into the hotel. That hotel being The Oak House, where we had first met.

Up in our room, I removed my dress to show the lovely bridal underwear underneath. I commented that there was confetti everywhere, hoping that My Boy would help to remove it. As I turned to face him, I saw that he'd passed out on the bed, fully dressed.

COME AND SEE THE SHOW OF THE CENTURY

STARRING

KATE DUGGAN

AND

TODD MORRIS

IN

"ONE WEDDING AND A RECEPTION"

A PRODUCTION IN TWO ACTS
ACT ONE. AXBRIDGE CHURCH
ACT TWO. AXBRIDGE TOWN HALL

HOWEVER

THIS PRODUCTION IS BEING PERFORMED ONLY ONCE

ON

SATURDAY THE FIFTH OF AUGUST 1995

AT THREE IN THE AFTERNOON

TICKET CONFIRMATION BY THE END OF JUNE TO
ANNE DUGGAN, 17 CHESTNUT AVENUE, AXBRIDGE
SOMERSET BS26 2ST. TELEPHONE 01934 733104

Supreme of Chicken Jean Bert

Ingredients

4x 6-8oz Chicken Supremes
8oz Button Mushrooms
6oz Prawns
1 Onion, finely chopped
½ pt White Wine
1 pt Chicken Volute
2 oz Butter
2 tbs Oil
¼ pt Double Cream
Seasoned Flour

Method

Slice the mushrooms finely and sweat off with the onion for five minutes.
Add the prawns and cook for a further 2 minutes.
Remove from the heat and place in a colander to drain.
Remove the fillet from the chicken supremes and flatten.
Slice into the supremes from the back to form a pocket and stuff with the mushroom and prawn mixture.
Replace the fillet inside the pocket to seal in the mixture.
Cover the supremes with seasoned flour.
Seal the supremes in the butter and oil and remove from the pan.
Add the remainder of the onion and lightly fry.
Add the wine and boil for 5 mins

Add the volute and simmer for 1 minute.
Replace the supremes in the pan and place in the oven at 350F for 20 mins.
Remove from the oven.
Check the consistency of the sauce and add the cream.
Stir in and pass the sauce back over the chicken.
Garnish with whole prawns.

Honeymoon

Our honeymoon was spent in a few locations. We did a bit of a road trip. I'd been doing an intensive driving course prior to the wedding. 3 weeks of lessons culminating in the test. I thought it'd be a good idea to do it then so I could drive on the honeymoon. It was one of my more stupid thoughts. Of course, I failed — in fact I didn't even turn up for the test as I was so far from ready. I've always done this. Take a really stressful time in my life and then see what other stresses I can throw at it. Never the easy path for Kate! Mostly I seem to manage to get through and succeed. But not this time. It actually took until 2005 until I passed my test. At one point I had 'learning to drive' in the hobbies and interests section of my CV as it was taking so long.

After our wedding night spent at the Oak House, (it was odd being there as customers not as staff) we had a night at Wood Hall, near Harrogate. Sarah had treated us to a night there and it was fantastic. Todd even managed to stay awake!!

We then spent a couple of days in Harrogate before driving up to Fort William in Scotland. We stayed in a little hotel for just over a week and explored the local area and mostly ate lovely food. We had planned to see lots of waterfalls but because of the heat, they'd dried up. Todd climbed Ben Nevis whilst we were staying there — of course he did. It was there! From the small amount of time he was away I think he must have run up and down that mountain with his camera slung across his body. He was buzzing when he returned and told me about the ice at the summit, despite the heat in the town. I wasn't totally static during the honeymoon, I did manage to 'Bag a Munro', although I'm not sure which one (I'm rubbish, I know). We came back via the Lake District. It was a very special time — like most people's honeymoons I suppose.

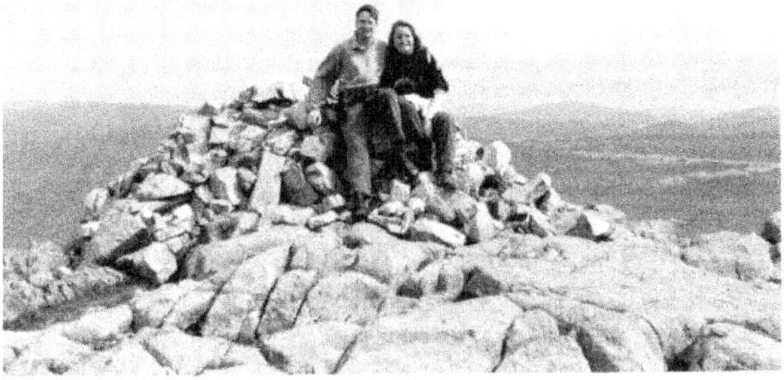

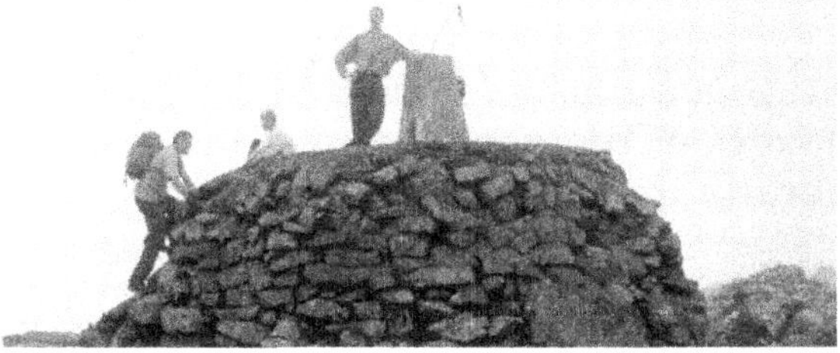

Monday 28th July 2003

Admitted to JR for operation.
Weight 69.5kg

Tuesday 29th July 2003

Palliative Gastric and Biliary bypass performed. There was a mobile mass at the head of the pancreas with multiple liver metastases in both lobes. There was no ascites and there was no peritoneal metastases. Cholecystectomy was performed. A roux loop of jejunum was constructed. Hepatico jejunostonomy and gastric jejunostomy were performed. He made an uneventful post operative recovery.

ASCITES; a build-up of fluid between the two layers of the peritoneum. This is a membrane that lines the abdomen.

CHOLECYSTECTOMY; the surgical removal of the gallbladder.

JEJUNOSTONOMY; the surgical creation of an opening through the skin at the front of the abdomen and the wall of the jejunum (part of the small intestine).

Dr Shackleton receives letter from Todd's employers requesting further information about his illness.

We were meant to be at Rick Stein's restaurant in Padstow for lunch. Cancelled.

Wednesday 30th July 2003

Dr Shackleton returns form to insurance company.

Thursday 31st July 2003

Should have been returning from Bude today.

Sunday 3rd August

In the real world we were due to go to Bulgaria for two weeks holiday.
Cancelled.
Diary; 1 mug of iced water

My diary - Sunday 1pm

I'm watching a programme about giraffes. David Attenborough said that because of high blood pressure their ankles should be very swollen. And it made me think of Todd and his poor swollen feet. They were huge at the end and must have been so painful. I tried to stop the skin cracking by rubbing cream into them. Sometimes it was OK, but other times I hurt him. Another thing to get wrong.

He couldn't get his slippers on properly and they left huge indentations when he did. In the end he had Tubi-grips instead. I still smell the cream from time to time. It reminds me. A sort of double-edged sword – seeing his cold, swollen feet on one hand, but at the same time remembering the feel of his skin.

I love him.

Six Weeks Later

Exactly six weeks after the wedding Todd and I went to his step-mother, Pat's birthday party. There was ten-pin bowling. I'd never done it before and I wasn't very good. And as I came off the back of the 'run' I tripped over a little step and fell flat on my face. Unfortunately, I also fell flat on my knee and it dislocated completely, the joint actually pushing out of the back of my leg. Todd leapt to my rescue and managed to put it part way back in, but not fully. The ambulance was called and I was stretchered away.

The first thing I remember hearing was someone telling me to stop swearing as I lay face down, unable to move!

I ended up in plaster for months. It went from the top of my thigh to my ankle and was completely straight as they couldn't get the knee to bend at all at the hospital. When I had the initial plaster cast put on, Todd kept using the gas and air every time the nurse left the room. He was getting a lovely little hit off it!

We were still living in the flat at the time — on the top floor. I had to travel up and down on my bum. Needless to say, I didn't go out much over those few months.

Todd was working hard (he always did) so I had to manage alone quite a bit. I learnt what I could carry with my crutches and learnt what I had to ask for before he went out. I got used to washing my hair in the kitchen sink and eating meals in there, standing up, as I couldn't carry a plate through to the table. And people called round to help when they could, especially my mummy.

Todd was never very good with ill people. He did whatever I asked of him but I could see his frustration.

It wasn't the first time I'd had knee problems. They'd started when I was 19, during the Imago year. In fact, the first time my knee dislocated was when I came offstage having performed my first one-woman play. I jumped up and down with excitement and my knee popped out. When the rest of Imago came backstage, they found me in tears and thought I was just being emotional, when in fact I was in agony!

I soon found out that I had kneecaps that liked to dislocate. They were always popping in and out of joint (apparently, I had high, small patellas that were laterally dislocatable!). I usually had to wear a Tubigrip on both knees. But this was the first time that I'd had a major problem because of them. I'd had a knee operation in 1993 which had been somewhat debilitating but no plaster casts before. It was a frustrating time for both of us.

Subject: a difficult day
Send: Tue, 01 Jun 2004 04:25:42 +0000

im having a hard day.

todd went into hospital for the first time a year ago today. we didn't have a clue what would happen. the day before he had driven down to collect me from my mum's house in somerset and then we went to see jo brand doing her stand-up show in oxford.

it's all very vivid and all very hard to re-live.

i miss him so much.

there are a lot of these anniversaries coming up.

im going to walk down to the sea and try to think of happy times.

kate
xx

Back To Work

After the plaster cast came off, my leg wouldn't bend. It was also a lovely greying colour. Very attractive. It took 2 or 3 sessions of physio each week to get it working again. Painful sessions that made me cry and get frustrated. Slowly, I managed to progress from crutches to a stick, but I still found the stairs really hard. I remember being terrified in a supermarket once because I was convinced that I was going to get knocked and my knee would come hurtling out of joint again. So, the thought of returning to a school environment wasn't really tempting. Adults might manage to avoid the woman with the stick but hundreds of teenagers might not be so aware.

I needed a change. I'd met Andrew doing Sunshine Radio. He worked in Bristol for the Civil Service and told me that they were looking for staff all the time. I went up for an interview and got the job as an Admin Assistant. It was a data entry job. Andy offered to car share and my new career began!

Data entry wasn't very exciting. Not very exciting at all in fact. I would set myself challenges about how many forms I could input onto the system in an hour, a morning, a day. It passed the time. The money was appalling but it was easy and I liked most of the people. Mary was hilarious. I loved her ever-changing hair colours and passion for cheese scones. She became a very good buddy. And so did Phil. Another top girl — although lots quieter. The other data entry people were also fab. We used to laugh a lot. We discovered a love of retro sweeties and surreal conversations. We decorated our little room and played music, quietly (obviously). We did get into trouble fairly frequently by being too rowdy or silly. One time, we had each emptied a whole packet of Fizz Wizz into our mouths when our supervisor came in. She had come in to collect our completed forms but decided to stay and talk to me — as I was the sensible one. As I answered her questions, I attempted to contain the fizzing, popping sweets within my mouth. It wasn't entirely successful. Especially when a piece shot out and pinged loudly against the can of Coke on my desk. She just looked a little confused and wandered off. The whole room exploded, with laughter and popping candy.

Because the office worked flexi-time, sometimes I'd be there with just my data entry buddies for company. The place would be deserted. Most civil servants preferred to start early and finish early. But if I was staying in Bristol with Mary to go out for the night I would work late. Well, I say work. More often than not we would wheel out our chairs into the corridor which was conveniently sloping. We'd push our chairs to the top of the slope and then chair-race back down again. Then we'd return to the office and spin each other round and round, whilst flicking the switch that let the chair down at the same time. We liked to feel dizzy!

Surprisingly, I got promoted whilst I was there. I think it was mostly because I did more work and I turned up most days.

It was lots of travelling and not much money, but the people made it worth it. It's always about the people, isn't it?

Monday 4th August 2003

Todd discharged from hospital so he can celebrate our 8th wedding anniversary tomorrow. Analgesia converted from IV Morphine via patient-controlled analgesia (PCA) to 160mg MST bd, using 50-60mls Oramorph for breakthrough pain. He also recommenced regular Paracetamol and Amitriptyline.
District nurse team advised of his return home and also notified community Macmillan nurse. Oncology dept pause further chemo pending further evaluation.

Diary; Oramorph 50ml @ 9.50pm and again @ 10.30pm

Tuesday 5th August 2003

Our 8th wedding anniversary.
Diary; MST upped to 400mg per day
Dad and Pat visit
Oramorph 30mg @ 5pm
Sick @ 11pm
Bamboo 42"

Wednesday 6th August 2003

See District Nurse
See Dr Shackleton
Patient remains very tired. Referred pain to right shoulder recurred as they stopped Amitriptyline in

hospital. Improved now has restarted but still some pain so to increase to 20mg for the moment.

Discussed need for employer's report. Still had ideas of being able to return to work but this is not realistic as he agreed. Discussed likelihood of significant fatigue and other problems being a continued issue, which won't go away. Doesn't want to see report despite what it says in the employer's letter. He is still unrealistic about the prognosis. Hopefully has moved forward on this a bit after this chat. Cancer diagnosis discussed. Patient's pruritus the same – fewer symptoms on Piriton.

Recurrence of constipation. Advised to add in Fybogel if restarting laxatives doesn't sort it out. Had increased Lactulose to 30ml and Senna. Lots of wind problems today. Probably as Lactulose and bowels recovering post-op.

Patient's nausea the same. Managing to drink but still vomiting 1-2 times a day. Passing wind lots. No laxatives in hospital. Has increased MST to 200mg x2 a day. Has spoken to Kate – Macmillan nurse – was advised Maxalon 4x a day instead of 3. Hopefully will improve as bowel function improves too.

Examination of patient. Generally, mildly tender abdomen. Upper abdomen and liver soft. Liver difficult to feel as large scar across upper abdomen. Bowel sounds active.

Diary; Sick @ 5.20am

Pete and Ellie visit, followed by Kim

Thursday 7th August 2003

Diary; Sick @ 1.20am
Oramorph 30mg vial @ 1am
Kevin and Rosie visit, followed by Dad and Pat.
Kate visits counsellor.

Friday 8th August 2003

Dr Shackleton replies to employer's query (charged at £36)
Todd's stitches come out
Diary; Oramorph 2 x 30mg vials @ 1am

Saturday 9th August 2003

Diary; Mum visits.
Oramorph 2 x 30mg vials @ 11.30am.

Sunday 10th August 2003

Diary; Kim and family visit.
Oramorph 2 x 30mg vials @ 4pm

My diary - Monday 10am

I woke up feeling guilty. I dreamt of Todd's funeral, although it wasn't as it actually happened. It was the 'do' afterwards and I slapped him across the face – twice. I felt bad. Then it made me smile.

Odd Socks

Todd always wore odd socks. One blue and one yellow. One green and one red. More often than not they had holes in.

I don't know why he wore odd socks. He just did.

Subject: Kate gets cultured!
Send: Wed, 09 Jun 2004 09:56:06 +0000

hi everyone

im still in sydney....enjoying having my own place! i've been fairly relaxed over the last couple of weeks....exploring the city and its surrounds.

i managed to get a half price trip to the blue mountains last week...a last minute deal which included a trip to a wildlife park....koala's fur is rougher than i expected! and i hand-fed a kangaroo....awww! then we went up into the mountains...which really are blue....due to the eucalyptus oil from the trees. spectacular views! lunch was included, then we went to karoomba and took the scenic railway down to the base. no-one told me it was the steepest railway in the world!! basically you travel in an open carriage down a sheer cliff in the dark...hurrah!! after a wander round the rainforest we went up to the top again on a sort of cable car. more views, then a drive back to sydney via the olympic park. then finally a cruise back to sydney harbour. a good day out! especially as it was tipping down when i left home b4 7am. as the morning progressed it brightened up and ended up being a beautiful day with a stunning sunset.

ive been to the theatre again. this time i saw 2 plays....kick the bucket (experimental!!) and intant karma (good story, problem with tone...was it meant to be funny or serious?) whilst there i met a real aussie! she is called michaeley and she is a writer for tv (blue heelers, etc) and has written a play which was read at a play reading the week b4. we chatted for ages and i ended up going to a play reading with her on monday. it was an interesting process. the actors had had 4 hours rehearsal time and the audience listened to it then had a discussion. i was brave...i joined in!

yesterday i went to a modern art exhibition at the museum of contemporary art. it was very thought provoking. some of it was amazing...some was complete pants!! then i went to see 'supersize me'...the film about the guy who eats mcdonalds for 30 days. that was also very thought provoking. very grim, but very funny. put me right off my big mac!!

at the weekend i went over to manly on the ferry. its where the sydeysiders go to the seaside. it was great. there was a food and wine festival on so that was also v good! i think it deserves another visit when its a bit quieter.

im planning a trip to melbourne on the 24th june. then im off on the great coast road to adelaide and then onto kangaroo island.

ive booked to go to the theatre again on friday....to see 'the flats' and 'vampirella'.

so, there's a snapshot of some of the things ive been up to recently. now im off to watch big brother aussie style...much the same as home except they have bizarre names....so far the evictees have been called aphrodite, igor, krystal and elle. this week we are expecting merlin to leave!

lots of love kate keep in touch xxx

Experiments

During my time as a data entry clerk, I realised I was nearer 30 than 20 and decided to live a little. Like I've said, I'd been sensible for years — playing at houses rather than going to house parties. I wasn't totally dull but I certainly hadn't ever been a wild child.

Todd and I started going out clubbing more (mostly with Mary and her bloke, Simon) and experimenting at the same time. We tried Acid, Ecstasy and Speed. For a while Speed became our drug of choice for clubbing. It gave us loads of energy and meant we could keep going all night. The come-down became increasingly crappy though and in the end, we stopped as the bad part was lasting days longer than the good night out.

Todd's dancing style had always been rather like Kevin Rowland from Dexy's Midnight Runners — lots of hands behind the back and foot stamping going on. I once suggested he loosen up and use his arms more. Moments later his flailing arms caught me across the face and I cut my lip. He was really embarrassed and I was bleeding. I never advised him on his dancing technique again!

Monday 11th August 2003

Diary; Mum visits, followed by Dad and Pat, followed by Mummy, Kevin and Panda.
Oramorph 2 x 30mg vials @ 2.30pm and again @ midnight.

Tuesday 12th August 2003

Diary; Panda visits and does reflexology.
Tom Wood visits.
Oramorph 2 x 30mg vials @ 3.30pm.

Wednesday 13th August 2003

District nurse visits. Todd is suffering from vomiting with trapped wind. Constipated and sore tail end/piles.
Dad and Pat visit, followed by Kim.
Oramorph 2x 30mg vials @ 12.30pm
1x 30mg @ 2pm and again @ 7pm.

Thursday 14th August 2003

Diary; Upped MST to 250mg twice daily.

Friday 15th August 2003

Liver clinic Outpatients appointment. Review following palliative bypass. Unfortunately, Todd is

not doing very well. He has got severe back pain which is poorly controlled despite escalation doses of MST. He is not able to eat much and has lost some weight. His abdominal wound is healing well and there is no evidence of any surgical complications. But his disease does appear to be progressing.
Referral to dietician.

Diary; weight 62.2kg.
Oramorph 60mg @ 10.30am, again @ 4.30pm and also @ 9.30pm.
Sick @ 6pm and @ 8pm.
Ate; crunchy nut cornflakes, toast and pate, Ensure milkshake, Build Up chicken soup, a piece of chocolate.

Saturday 16th August 2003

Diary; Oramorph 60mg @ 10am and @ 12.30pm
Hiccups 3 times
Ate; crunchy nut cornflakes, biscuit, 2 bits chocolate, prawn cocktail, biscuit, 4 Pringles.

Sunday 17th August 2003

Diary; Oramorph 60mg @ 11am and @ 5pm
Ate; crunchy nut cornflakes, cheese and tom sandwich, ice lolly, strawberry milkshake, 2 biscuits, strawberry milkshake, carrots.

My diary - Thursday 1.30pm

I went to a memorial lunch for Todd yesterday at his workplace, with Jackie. I was amazed. They'd gone to so much trouble. The restaurant was decorated and there were posters and photos on the walls and tables. The staff had all dressed up in Rocky Horror Show gear. When I first saw it all, I burst into tears and ran out. But I knew I owed it to Todd to pull myself together.

The restaurant was mobbed. They had a raffle and had also been collecting for Cancer Research for a while. Hilary phoned me today to say that they had raised £452 yesterday, with more to come. (I had a letter from the funeral directors too – saying that they had raised £578.15 through donations. A total of £1030.15. That's amazing. I'm so proud of him. But who gave the 15p?!)

I was very proud yesterday. He had obviously affected a lot of people at work. I had big problems with my feelings towards the company earlier in the year. I was disgusted by their sickness policy. One-week sick pay, no discussion allowed. It wasn't as if he just had flu, was it? So, I was angry about that and didn't know if I wanted to go along yesterday because of it. I'm glad I did though as it was the company that was crap, not the staff. If I'd known it was a Rocky Horror event I'd have dressed up! Well, maybe not the full outfit and make-up. I'd also have taken some photos along of Todd in his gear…he always looked amazing in stockings and suspenders! Never mind, doesn't matter really. I posted some in today instead. They had the video playing and a CD of the music. I had to show them how to Time Warp properly.

They had 'Andy the Chef' in to do Deli A Go-Go (shockingly bad name). He and Todd used to be a bit of a double act whenever he visited. They had the same sense of humour and naughty little boy behaviour. He was very sweet. Joking and fun during the lunch, but very kind afterwards. That's hard when you have a white face and black lips, not to mention a half-mask. He had been working with the chef, Nick Nairn, in Scotland recently and he got me a signed book from him, dedicated to Todd, 'top chef'.

I also collected his stuff. I'm glad he gave me a list of what was there because I wouldn't have had a clue. I managed to sell them the cash register and some pans, which was a relief. There is a lot of catering gear to sell. I don't really know what to do with it. Kim said he will help me with it, which is also quite a relief.

I hate getting rid of Todd's things. It seems all wrong. Nasty. I know he talked about it, but even so it's a difficult thing. I hate that so much of this is revolving around money. Not good.

Tom is coming up later. He is buying Todd's car. I'm not sure how I feel about it. It needs selling. I can't drive it and I have my Mini for when I pass my test. I could keep it, it would be more reliable than mine. But it seems too grown-up for me. Not a first car. It's not as if Todd had it for very long, he only bought it in March. So, it doesn't have particular memories attached to it. I think it will still be hard though. Everything is hard, so why wouldn't this be the same?

Relocation, Relocation, Relocation

Whilst I was eating popping candy and having chair races, Todd was getting increasingly frustrated at the Arosfa. He'd been there 9 years and had the kitchen running smoothly. He'd trained Wayne and had him as his 2nd chef and they worked really well together. But it wasn't challenging him creatively. He needed a change.

Nigel, the restaurant manager, had moved to Oxfordshire a couple of years previously to work at Williams Grand Prix. He kept in touch with Todd and told him they were looking for a new chef to provide the catering at their conference centre. They wanted someone self-employed. After a lot of deliberation Todd became that chef. He'd already established Todd's Katering (see what he did there?!) and done some function work in the Weston area, doing dinner parties in people's homes, providing buffets for parties, etc. But this was a different league.

He inherited the menus from the outgoing catering company, but delivered them his way. Gradually he changed the menus to be his own, retaining some of the original items and introducing new things. Mostly he was providing upmarket buffets — hot and cold finger food.

To start with he had to use the staff canteen to cook the hot food and use a sort of hostess trolley to bring it back to the conference centre. What was mad was that he'd have to wheel the trolley through the highly prestigious Williams F1 museum. To start with it was distracting but it became run of the mill — shooting past thousands of pounds worth of Grand Prix memorabilia with a trolley full of miniature beef Wellingtons, Cajun chicken and samosas.

When he was starting up, I worked with him too. I did a lot of sandwich-making. I was probably more of a hindrance than a help as I wasn't particularly fast at that point. I did speed up a bit years later when we opened Cheeky Monkeys, a sandwich bar which I ran. It was a short-lived venture. Unfortunately, the Foot and Mouth crisis started and being a market town, it became deserted. No people coming to town meant no customers, meant no money, meant no Cheeky Monkeys. It was a shame but just one of those things. You don't know until you try.

Back at Williams, Todd was a changed man. He loved his work. Most days he had very early starts but he was his own boss. He didn't work evenings and only rarely at weekends. He was no longer angry with waiting staff. He was light-hearted, singing and whistling (he'd always been a 'musical' chef, but it increased tenfold!). He also brought Wayne up to work with him.

His work challenged him and he was constantly improving his food and what he offered. His range of biscuits became very popular. He sold kilos of them.

Then they introduced Race Days at the conference centre. Customers would come in and watch the Grand Prix on massive screens, visit the museum, have a talk with some Williams big-wigs and eat fantastic food all day (or all night, depending on where the race was being held). He was very busy but very content.

His job also enabled him to indulge in his hobbies. He played squash regularly and ran occasionally but his great passion became kayaking. He'd started when we were living in Weston, paddling out to sea from time to time. But once we moved to Oxfordshire, he became obsessed. He became a keen member of the Kingfisher Canoe Club in Abingdon. He'd spend hours at pool sessions and out on the Thames. Then there were the trips all over the country. I became a canoe widow. I wasn't interested in trying it out (too much of a wuss!) but met his new friends from time to time. It seemed to be a hobby that attracted people from all walks of life. He became the one with loads of friends, the total opposite of how it used to be. I found it hard fitting into that area but he slotted right in.

He also trained to be a canoe coach. He'd always loved teaching people in his kitchen and this was an extension of that. He was a natural. He progressed through the levels and became a level 4 paddler and a level 2 coach. Another element of his life that he loved.

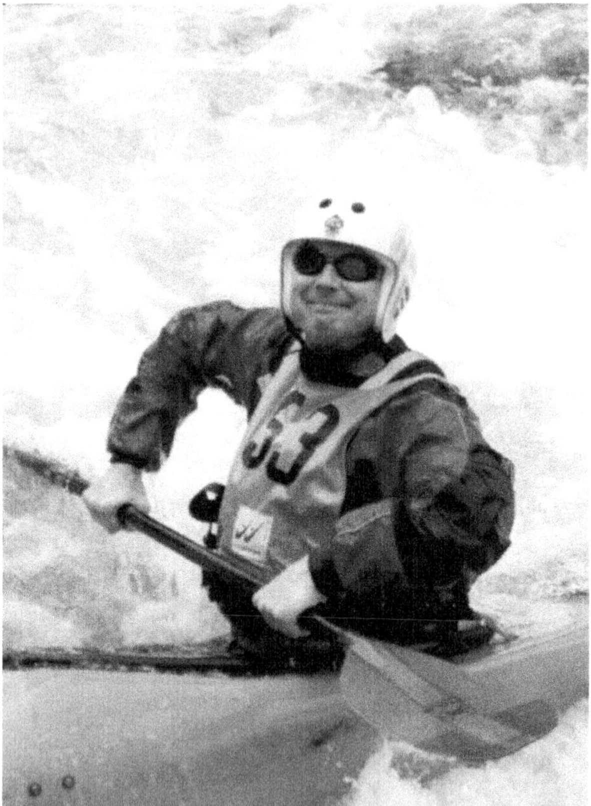

Biscuit Mix

Ingredients

2 lb Butter
2 lb Icing Sugar
2 Eggs
3 lb Plain Flour

Method

Cream the butter and sugar together
Add the eggs.
Beat in the flour, until the mix leaves the sides of the bowl.
(To this mix a large variety of flavourings can be added, eg. Cocoa, chocolate chips, walnut halves, coconut, ginger – dried or stem -, cinnamon, etc, etc, etc)
When you have mixed in your flavourings (the mix can be divided up to make up to 6 flavours) roll into tubes approx 1 ½ thick and place in the fridge for 2 hours.
Once chilled, cut into ¼ inch slices.
These biscuits are now ready to bake, on a greased tray at 175C until golden.

You can also freeze the biscuit mix until required.

Evesham Hotel

21st April 1998. We celebrated 10 years of being together. We had lots of anniversaries through the year, but this one was to celebrate when we began. It was my favourite.

I'd seen an advert for the Evesham hotel and thought it sounded fairly mad, so we booked in for a weekend. It was indeed bonkers, and remained so each time we visited. Some of the bedrooms had themes to them (I remember staying in the Eygptian room, the attention to detail was great. It was all very tongue in cheek). We'd always try to peek into other rooms to see what they were like.

Each key fob had a bear on it. These bears had names so you would ask for them rather than a room number at Reception. You can see why I'd appreciate the place! And the food was stunning. There were rubber ducks by the baths and waterproof activity books to fill in. It was a crazy place, full of stuff and we loved it. We visited quite a few times. On our final wedding anniversary, I promised Todd, I would take him there again, but we never made it.

Monday 18th August 2003

Visited Doctor's surgery. Hiccough symptoms, worse in evenings. Generally, very bright and chatty.

Diary; increased MST to 300mg twice daily.
Oramorph 60mg @ 7.30am and @ 6pm
4am hiccups and trapped wind from Hell.
Ate; crunchy nut cornflakes, bread with pate and jam, 2 biscuits, 6oz sirloin steak, choc mousse and cream.

Tuesday 19th August 2003

Dietician
Weight 62.2kg
BMI 20kg/m2
Patient advised to have small frequent energy dense meals, snacks and drinks throughout the day. In addition, prescribable products for nutrition support have been recommended. Plans to see patient at next outpatient appt.

1pm phone chemo suite to check whether it's going ahead

3pm chemo restarts

Diary; 8.30am POO AGH
9.30am POO AGH
10am 60mg Oramorph
10.30am 30mg Oramorph
Midday 30mg Oramorph

3.30pm 60mg Oramorph
7pm 120mg Oramorph
Evening POO AHA
Ate; crunchy nut cornflakes, bacon, cheese and mushroom Panini, bounty bar, raspberry milkshake, lamb stew.

Wednesday 20th August 2003

Diary; 1am Barfed up trapped wind
9.30am – 2pm slept
6.30pm 120mg Oramorph
10pm sick
10.30 120mg Oramorph
Ate; rice crispies, milk shake, 2 poached eggs on bread, 3 biscuits, 10 sweets.

Thursday 21st August 2003

11.30am appointment with Dr Bee Wee, Consultant in Palliative Medicine at Sobell House (hospice)
At the clinic, Mr Morris' main problems were twofold. First, he had moderate to severe epigastric pain which was typical of pancreatic cancer pain. Fortunately, this remains sensitive to morphine. The current dose of MST 300mg b.d. is obviously not containing his pain any longer. He requires between 120-240mg Oramorph each day for breakthrough pain. I have therefore increased his MST to 400mg b.d. Whilst this may seem a relatively high dose, he is clearly tolerating this well and his pain does respond to Morphine.

However, thinking ahead, I thought it might be helpful to involve my colleagues at the Pain Relief unit sooner rather than later. If they were able to offer him a coeliac block or equivalent neuro-anaesthetic procedure, and if it were to be successful, it could improve his pain control considerably and reduce his opioid requirements. The other problem that he is currently experiencing is vomiting.
Increased Morphine and Metoclopramide to alleviate pain and sickness. Consultant writes to GP and pain relief unit at the Churchill hospital.
GP. Chat with patient. No more hiccoughs. Urine tests done.

Bought remote controlled aeroplane

Diary; midday Oramorph 120mg
Increase MST to 800mg daily and double dose Metoclopramide.
Ate; cornflakes, beans on toast with cheese, 2 biscuits, lamb stew, milkshake x2, choc sponge and custard.

Friday 22nd August 2003

Appointment with Moira from SAAFA (ex-servicemen's support), helpful with suggestions on ways forward and financial assistance.

Diary; 1.30pm sick
Kim visits
Ate; cornflakes, brie wedges, 8 sweets, 1 scone.

Saturday 23rd August 2003

Diary; Sarah visits
Ate; weetabix, chicken flan, roast lamb.

Sunday 24th August 2003

Diary; Sarah visiting
Mum visits
Uffington White Horse Show
3pm Oramorph 120mg
Trapped wind all night (vomited)
Ate; 2 weetabix, 2 toast, little lunch, 2 rock cakes.

My diary - Wednesday 1pm

I haven't written for a few days. I'm not sure why. Tom came and collected the car. We had to go to Oxford to change the tax disc back from a disabled one to a normal one. Yet another thing that isn't straight forward. We also went to the cinema. We saw 'Love Actually', which was very good. I kept wondering how Todd would have reacted to it. Moaned about going to a chick-flick, eaten popcorn noisily in the quiet bits, maybe dropped off, but enjoyed the totty probably.

I told him about it. I talk to him a lot at the moment. I know he's not really there but it's comforting, for a moment.

I didn't see anyone at the weekend. On Saturday I didn't even talk to anyone which was very strange.

I took my theory test on Monday. Third time lucky, I passed. I'd been revising for an hour a day for a while. I'm not sure how I would have reacted if I hadn't passed this time. I think I may have given up totally. Then I went to the cinema on my own in the afternoon. It was fine. Lots of single people go to matinees.

Then yesterday I went into school which was very scary. I seem to have agreed to try to start to go back. Observing lessons first and then a reduced timetable next term.

Joe came round last night to get the instructions about how to look after the animals whilst I'm away. He was talking about Todd's boat and paddles. He will sell them for me through the canoe club. I know they won't rip me off, the opposite really.

I'm off to Lille tomorrow with Sarah. I'm really in two minds about it. I'm looking forward to it as a chance to explore a new place and do something pleasant. But at the same time, I'm really wound up. I'm scared about being away from home. It's the first time I've spent a night away. And I feel guilty about doing a nice thing. I don't feel I deserve it. I don't deserve to have a good time when Todd isn't here to share it with me. I also feel that it won't go well. I don't trust that anything good can happen to me.

ForniKate

Whilst Todd was creating his empire at Williams I had got a new job in Abingdon. It was administration again for a company called Blick. I didn't even consider teaching at this point in my life – I really didn't think I could do it. After a while I'd been promoted and later, I would be promoted again, so that I would be running the admin team. It wasn't too bad. The work was pretty mundane but the people kept it interesting (as always) and we had a lot of laughs there. But I also spent a lot of time being seriously unhappy. It wasn't exactly a creative breeding ground. Clocking-in machines, CCTV and fire alarms weren't particularly inspiring.

Yet, I began writing again. Perhaps because I was unhappy and needed to escape – who knows? That used to be the case, that I'd only ever write when I was really down. Not so anymore, thankfully.

Each lunchtime I'd go off to the conference room, eat my lunch and then write solidly for 30 minutes. And that's how 'Daphne is Dancing' got written; my first full-length monologue. I hadn't written it for a purpose. But once it was finished, I started wondering what to do with it. But not very much.

Months later I decided I would take it to the Edinburgh Festival. I don't know where the idea came from but I was suddenly certain that that's what I would do. I knew nothing about how to go about it, (which was probably a good thing. If I'd known what I was letting myself in for I don't think I would have bothered) but I had a bee in my bonnet. Kate was going to Scotland. I do this sometimes, decide something will occur and set about making it happen, not knowing where the idea came from in the first place, just like my trip to Australia.

I got the information I needed from the Festival organisers and found a venue to book. It was the back room of a pub – The Holyrood Tavern. It had a small capacity, it wasn't really central and the only available slots were late afternoon or very late at night. I decided the afternoon slot would be better. I felt the late night one would be full of really drunk people and I wouldn't be able to handle it.

It was probably the wrong decision as a saucy show at tea-time wasn't ideal either. People weren't in that frame of mind at that point in the day it seemed. But I could have got into all sorts of bother late at night. Rock and a hard place spring to mind. It was what I could afford.

It seemed that once the venue was booked, there was an endless demand for money to be spent out. I wasn't earning much. Not enough to bankroll this project certainly. A few people said they would chip in — they knew how much I wanted to perform. And then it got suggested that I got sponsored to do the show. It wasn't for charity, it was for me, everyone knew that. And cheques started coming in from family, friends and work colleagues. I couldn't have done it without those generous people — especially Malcolm Spratt. With the money worries slightly allayed I started rehearsing. I'd decided to put 'Daphne is Dancing' with a play I'd performed previously called 'The Same Old Story', by Dario Fo and Franca Rame. In fact, the series of monologues it came from — Female Parts — was probably what made me start writing one-woman plays in the first place. I'd been performing the play on and off for years for fun. It was a political piece, heavily feminist. But it was really funny, absurd and rude. It started with me on my back with my feet behind my head, having uncomfortable sex. Whilst wearing a tutu!

Together with Daphne, it would become 'ForniKate' — my show at The Holyrood Tavern for 16 nights during August 1999.

I started learning lines and rehearsing. I was lucky that work let me use the empty warehouse space to rehearse in. It was just being used for storage by then. My stage area was marked out on the floor and as I was a key-holder I could lock up the building on my way out in the evening. Everyone knew what I was doing but some found it stranger than others. I'd turn round from time to time and see little faces watching me with bemused expressions. One colleague managed to talk the local council into giving me a municipal rubbish bin to be used in Daphne (it was set at a festival, so an over-flowing bin was very appropriate)

My mate Garry, who I'd known since Central, was going to be my techie. I was doing everything else, but I couldn't physically do my own lighting and sound! He started visiting Oxfordshire regularly to give an outside eye. That was invaluable, as it's really hard to direct yourself completely.

August came round and Garry and I set off for Edinburgh on separate flights. Todd had paid for mine with Air Miles he'd collected with all his Sainsbury's shopping.

After the technical rehearsals were completed and my nerves settled down, I settled into a routine of standing on the Royal Mile in the day, handing out flyers and then performing in the late afternoon. Evenings were quiet affairs. I was staying with Dot, my sister's best friend, and Garry was in a hostel in town (complete with bed bugs!). He made lots of new friends – he was a seasoned traveller. But I'd go back to the house and watch Corrie! My family came to visit during my stay too. And Dot put them all up too – bless her!

The only one who was notable for his absence was Todd. He was just too busy with work to make the long trip over the border. I missed him. I'd wanted him to be proud of what I'd achieved.

Mind you, The Scotsman didn't think I should be proud. As a small-scale show I only received one review at the Festival – on the Page of Shame!

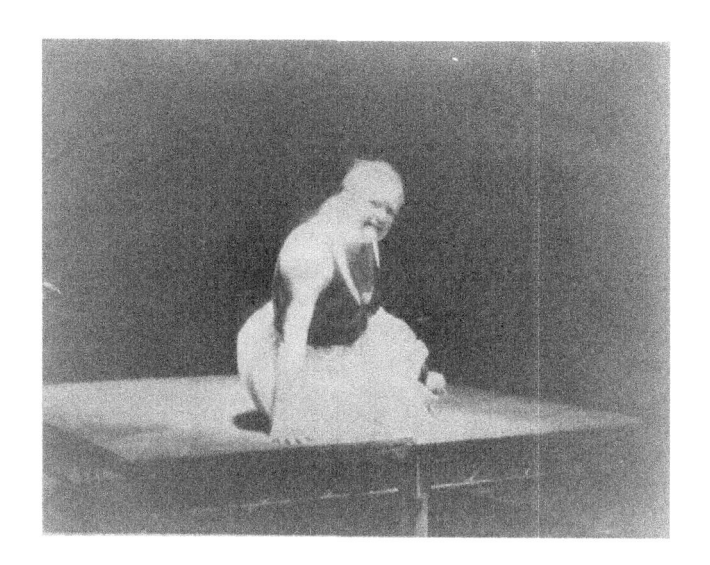

Subject:

Send: Fri, 02 Jul 2004 02:15:07 +0000

hello everyone

well, im back in adelaide again. sorry ive not written for a while, but ive been quite busy and not near a computer! so sit back, sip the beverage of your choice and enjoy the (probably random and long-winded) tales of the last couple of weeks.

i did manage to get up early and catch the train to canberra. everyone said it would be freezing down there, so i wrapped up warm. but it was just like a lovely autumn day back home...sunny and crisp...i was much too hot! ho hum! the journey down there was very pretty. and ive discovered a very good thing about train travel...you can be really nosy and look into people's back yards and be hugely judgmental!!

canberra itself was an odd place. there didnt seem to be any people there! just lots of open spaces. it didnt feel like a city at all. and considering it is the capital, it only has one platform at the train station. i visited a film and sound archive...a national one no less! (everything was the 'national' something or other there!) it turned out to be about the size of a museum you would find in weston-super-mare!

then i visited parliament house and experienced question time. i saw the prime minister, john howard, there. he didnt seem particularly involved...just kept swinging on his chair!

i spent that weekend with george and fay. we went to friends for supper on saturday night. we played the 20th anniversary edition of trivial pursuit....how can it have been around for so long? i remember when it first came out. oops sounding old now.,....i'll start commenting on how young policemen look these days in a minute! we ended up watching the germany v latvia match in the middle of the night....v odd! then on sunday, we went down to bondi for brunch and just slumped in front of the tv in the evening.

on monday i went to another play reading, which was ok. i got chatting to lots of people there. then on the tuesday i went to the sydney theatre and saw a big-scale production of a play called 'the unlikely prospect of happiness'. it was very good...very rude! but because it was a big theatre, i didnt get chatting to anyone.

on thursday i travelled down to melbourne on the train. it was delayed because of a suspected bomb scare. sounds very dramatic but wasnt at all! the trains here are very different from home...the food is edible for a start!

i stayed with sarah's friend, bev and her husband, phil in their flat at port melbourne. their flat is right on the waterfront...and is very smart. a great place to stay. i explored the city a little on friday. the thing i noticed most about melbourne was the sound of the place. the trams make a lot of noise..not unpleasant, just distinctive.

on saturday i got on my tour along the great ocean road. it was a four day trip and it was fantastic. i went with the same company as i did the red centre with. the route is really spectacular. its quite a twisty road, right by the ocean. sometimes it runs along by the beach, sometimes along the cliffs. some parts really reminded me of cornwall! after that section you drive through more pastoral land...more like devon! and finally, the land flattens out and turns into somerset!! v odd! very beautiful though. there were only 6 people in the group plus the driver. we all got very well...well, 5 of us did! the group even managed to go in the sea. the driver thought we were absolutely mad....the next land mass is the antarctic after all! but a dare is a dare!! we stayed in dorm accommodation in hostels so it was all a bit cosy! when we arrived in adelaide we decided to have a night out together...and what a night it turned out to be. i ended up getting back to my bed at about 4am...and had to get up at 5.30am to go on the next trip to kangaroo island. ouch! i did it though. the ferry crossing over to the island was appalling...really rough. i guess that was my pay back for my late night...i was SO ill!!! anyway, the island was lovely. the sea-lions, seals and rock formations were stunning! luckily the return journey yesterday was smoother...and i spent the entire journey up on the top deck looking at the disappearing horizon which helped! we got back to adelaide at about 11.30 last night and i then realised that the bus station was locked and therefore so was my luggage! i returned this morning to collect it and pay the excess charge....grrrr!!

im meeting some of the girls from my trips later today. we are going to visit the largest cinema complex in the southern hemisphere! yippee! movies and choc tops! and later im off to the cabaret festival to watch some bizarre performances which should be fun.

so there we are...up to date mostly! a busy couple of weeks, with some difficult bits and some fantastic bits.

ive also changed my flight home so im now coming back on 4th/5th august. that way i get the full 3 months.
speak soon. lots of love kate
xxx

It's Just A Jump To The Left

I'd been obsessed with the Rocky Horror Show since I was 13. I'd first seen the film late at night at home. I found myself Time-Warping at about 1am. About a year later my brother, Kevin, and his then girlfriend, Panda (later his wife) took me to see the live show in Bath. We dressed up but got it all a bit wrong. I particularly remember my brother in a safari suit! But I was stunned by the performance. I'd had my Rocky Horror cherry popped and I wanted more, more, more! At that point the show was touring a lot and I managed to see it in Bristol and Bath pretty frequently. I was dressing up properly by now and spent a lot of time creating elaborate make-up and back-combing my hair. Occasionally I'd go in a big group of people (Once was on a school trip. Lots of people got ready at my house and my Great Aunt Nora thought it was delightful as all these teenagers raced around in their skimpies whilst she stayed with my mum. We all proceeded to get on the school mini-bus!), but more often I'd go with Debs or Nicki.

Then I met Todd and popped his Rocky Horror cherry…fairly soon after he'd popped mine, I suppose! He took to it all like a duck to water. He was a very Sweet Transvestite! Often, he'd have his fags tucked down his stocking top − v glam.

He was so happy with his own sexuality that he wasn't at all phased when other blokes chatted him up and kissed him when we were at the theatre.

We were always introducing new people to the Rocky experience − taking 'virgins' along to the show. I still do it now. They would vary in their confidence towards dressing up. Wearing fishnets with a white shirt and suit jacket seemed to be a good half-way costume for a lot of people. Others didn't dress up at all, whereas some went the whole hog — Thea being a case in point. And she certainly had the arse for it!

Some friends took a lot of persuading. The funniest was Lee (Todd's kayaking buddy) who was persuaded into the shirt/jacket/stocking combo with the assurance that no-one would see him — it was dark, he was wearing make-up, etc. Tentatively he rolled on his fishnets. However, the Rocky Horror hadn't been to Oxford before and not many people had dressed up so those who had got noticed — especially by the local TV news team who were filming outside the door. Sorry Lee!

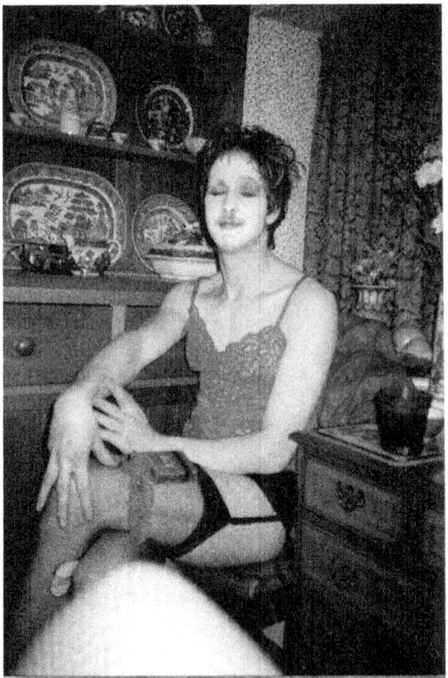

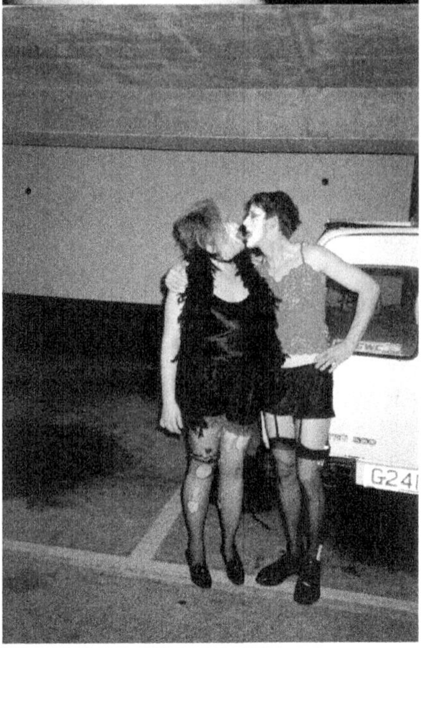

Monday 25th August 2003

Diary; first flight of remote-controlled plane. Climbed too steep and hit power line. Broke 1st wing.
Ate; cereal x2, soup and bread, fish pie.

Tuesday 26th August 2003

Diary; 8.30am Pete and Ellie collected us and took us to the Churchill Hospital.
9am Path labs – bloods taken
11am chemo starts
4pm vomit
Ate; cereal, cheese roll, jam doughnut, fish pie, 3 biscuits, Dime bar.

Wednesday 27th August 2003

See Doctor. Patient's condition the same. Hiccoughs gone. Chemo yesterday. Not sleeping very well. Wind waking him. Vomits alternate days. Appetite improved on Prednisolone (steroid) for past 2 weeks. Medication increased, is now taking Maxalon though not helped wind or nausea much. No side effects. Has increased MST to 400mg bd
Wind symptoms, mainly epi-gastric. Asilone helps but tends to bring it back up with the wind. Will try Deflatine tablets.
Backache symptoms. Orthopaedic exam. No spinal tenderness. Little pain on exam with the

MST, but slight tenderness just to left of low thoracic spine.

Diary; Dad and Pat visit
Anne visits
Kate to see Dr Robinson
6pm vomit
Ate; toast x2, prawn and avocado salad.

Thursday 28th August 2003

Pain clinic appointment. Alternative options discussed if MST ceased to work (epidurals, continuous epidurals and coeliac plexus blocks)

COELIAC PLEXUS BLOCK; **neurolytic coeliac plexus block is an effective method for relieving pain associated with pancreatic and non-pancreatic intra-abdominal malignancies, with approximately 90% of patients achieving at least partial pain relief short term (two weeks) and long term (three months and beyond). Neurolytic blocks, i.e. those which destroy the nerve, are only used in patients with short life expectancies or where other simpler techniques have failed.**

Increased Amitriptyline to help with sleep and also pain. Letter described him as a 'delightful young man'.

However, Todd was not happy as the appointment took ages and he was having a 'good day'. He wanted to make the most of it, not just go to hospital again.

Ate; cornflakes, Burger King bacon double cheeseburger and fries, banana, small dinner, lion bar, pudding.

Friday 29th August 2003

Diary; Kim visits
Ate; 5 biscuits, cornflakes, pizza, pork chop, croquette potatoes, meringue and cream.

Saturday 30th August 2003

Diary; Dad and Pat visit.
Ate; cornflakes, toast, pizza.

Sunday 31st August 2003

Visit Cotswold Wildlife Park with Jackie, John, Pat, Kim, Penny, Sam, Harry, Helen, Paul, Jennifer and Elizabeth.
Have a picnic and look at the animals. One of our favourite places.

My diary - Friday 10.30am

Again, I haven't written for a while. I think it's partly because I've been with people a lot over the last week. Sarah in Lille, and then Mummy.

Lille was nice. I got upset when we left the house. Sarah asked if I wanted to cancel the trip but I told her to 'just drive'. I felt a bit claustrophobic on the Eurostar but tried to divert my attention. During the daytime I was OK, keeping busy wandering around the town. I was more wobbly in the evenings. I got upset in a restaurant, but I don't think it was noticed. And I cried when I went to bed (I always do), but I didn't want to disturb Sarah, so I did it silently, both nights.

We stopped in London on the way back and stayed with Lesley and Steve. I think it was a bit of a mistake. They are a nice couple but I have only met them twice before. I just felt uncomfortable. I'd been away from home for enough time by then. Steve asked some difficult questions about returning to school. I felt very exposed. He seemed to think that I should share my grief with the students to make them better people. But I'm not a teaching resource. My grief is personal and if I want to share it, it has to be on my terms. Not because I've broken down in front of a group of teenagers.

Of course, I kept my true feelings hidden and sobbed when I went to bed. I couldn't stop. That was the first time for a while that the crying has been so uncontrollable.

I didn't enjoy London very much. It was all too busy. Too many people. Too much traffic. Too dirty.

Then Mummy arrived on Tuesday with Panda. Panda collected Tom's old car. So,
it's just the Mini outside now. It looks very strange. All lost and little.

I didn't really get upset in front of Mummy. Why am I hiding so much? I'm acting all the time. Is this what it will be like from now on? Acting with everyone and sobbing when I'm alone?

12.10pm

I've just come back from the Doctor. She has prescribed anti-depressants. I'm not sure how I feel about that. I don't want to get hooked. And I don't want to feel sedated and 'muffled'. Will I stop being me? Or be some reduced version of me? Apparently, they take about two weeks to work. I might get an upset stomach and I could feel increased anxiety and be a bit hyper. If I feel worse overall, I have to go back to the surgery. Shit.

House!

The year after Edinburgh, we eventually moved into a house. We'd been living in flats since we'd got together and we'd longed for the space that a house would give us. We were still renting but at least we could have all our belongings out; including our wedding presents. Since we'd first opened them in 1995, they had been in storage in Jackie's loft. It was like unwrapping them all over again. Very exciting!

At last, we could have people to stay in a proper spare room, with a bed. Not on a blow-up mattress on the floor. We had outside space too. And we had our own stairs on which we went up to bed. We had a utility room where the washing machine was – and a line. No more drying washing over the bath or on the radiators. We had a proper home at last. For the first time in years, it didn't feel like we were camping. It felt we had space to breathe. Space to dream. Well, for me anyway. I'd always been the dreamer; planning for the future. Todd was much more down-to-earth and rooted. He lived for the moment, and didn't generally get swept away by my flights of fancy.

Our home became the venue for parties and good times. It may have been an anonymous house on an estate, much like its neighbours. But our belongings made it special. It was ours.

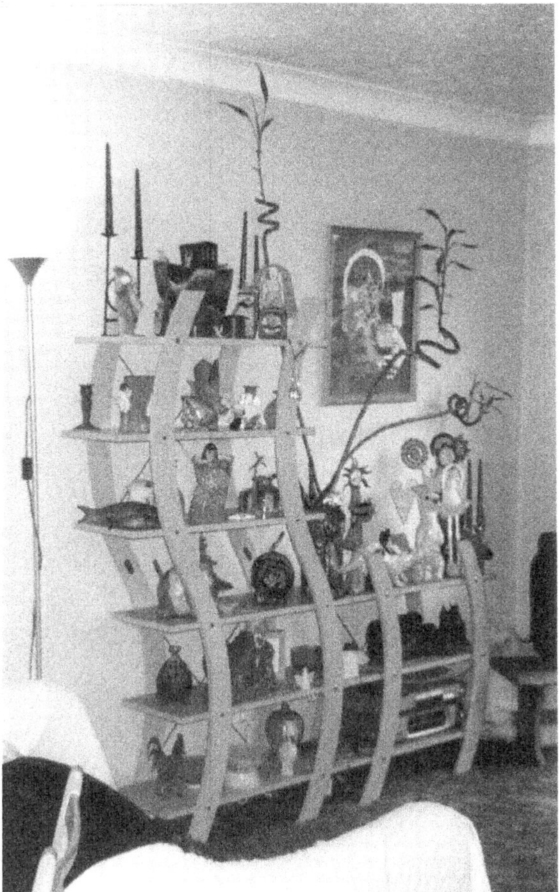

Medallions of Pork, with a white wine and mushroom sauce

Ingredients (serves 2)

12 oz Pork Medallions
½ Onion, finely chopped
8 oz Sliced Mushrooms
¾ pint White Wine
¾ pint Chicken Volute

Method

Sweat off onions, add the pork and seal both sides
Add the mushrooms and cook for 5 minutes.
Add the wine and reduce by half
Add the volute and simmer for 5 minutes
Remove the pork and correct the consistency.
Arrange the pork on plates and cover with the sauce.

Nobody's Perfect

Todd and I had a successful relationship for many years, almost 16 in fact. But it wasn't perfect. No-one's is, is it? We had lots of difficult times in amongst the good periods. We never really rowed — we were sulkers. There were times when there would be complete silence in our home as each of us held our ground and didn't give in. Eventually, after a few days, one of us would crack and apologise (more often than not, it would be me) — often not remembering what had caused the silence in the first place.

Other times, we'd just carry on living our lives, barely registering the other person. Taking each other completely for granted. Neither of us feeling special or cherished. Not feeling anything much really. Those were the most dangerous times as it only took some flattery from outside to make you re-consider your life and wonder what if? Like I said neither of us was perfect, but we forgave. And carried on. Getting stronger as a couple because of what had happened.

Monday 1st September 2003

Blood sample taken pre-chemo.
Sick note written for 3 months.

Tuesday 2nd September 2003

Chemotherapy 2.30pm.

Friday 5th September 2003

Blood transfusion given.

Saturday 6th September 2003

John and Pat collect us for the postponed trip to Bude. We stay at their house overnight.

Sunday 7th September 2003

Travel to Bude. Stay at Stratton Garden Hotel near Bude. Todd is exhausted by the journey. We sleep in a twin room at his request so he won't disturb me so much in the night. His sleep is very disturbed and he ends up watching TV, very quietly, at odd hours of the day and night.

My diary - 2am

All the bad stuff has come back again. I can't sleep and I can't stop visualising his last few days. It's all so unfair. He shouldn't have had to go through all that. We were so determined to get him home. But I didn't know how to cope when he got here. I didn't know what to expect, I suppose no-one could have told me, because no-one knew. But it was such a shock when his legs gave way. I didn't know how to help him up. Thank God Sarah was here and she managed to get him on his feet. But then it happened again, when I was supposed to be supporting him. He just dropped from under my arm and hit his head on the stairs. Again, I didn't know what to do. Between us, Sarah and I got him back to the settee. That was the last time he walked anywhere. I feel so guilty because that fall was my fault. I should have been able to support him. I called the doctor because his breathing was so difficult and I was so worried that he had hurt his head. He said that his head was fine and that his breathing was difficult because he'd used so much energy. All he wanted to do was go to the loo on his own, in private, with a bit of dignity.

After that he used the commode. He would only let me help him though, and that was fairly minimal. He really wanted independence right until the end. We'd try to make a joke of it, but it wasn't very funny.

After his falls, Sarah and I decided to stay up with him overnight too. Sarah sent me up to bed for four hours and then she went to bed after me. Of course, I couldn't really sleep. We got through the next day. His cousins visited with their partners. Too many people for too long. Todd slept through the visit. He woke as they were leaving and I think Scott saw me helping him to have a drink.

Sunday was another shared night. Sarah said that they talked quite a lot. Not about anything much but still chattered. Apparently, he was quite demanding. Lots of lemonade to drink and fags to smoke. Indoors now, of course.

He was quieter with me, but panicky because we'd run out of clear lemonade and only had the cloudy stuff. But I couldn't sort that out for him. Sarah had left and I couldn't leave him. His Dad went and got him some whilst he was here visiting.

I can't do this anymore. It hurts too much.

Carol

I met Carol during my time at Central and she quickly became a very good friend. She was an extremely focussed and driven young woman — she put a lot of us to shame. She had a really dark sense of humour, which developed as she got older. Not everyone 'got' Carol, she could be quite prickly and she didn't like to let people get close to her. That didn't fit in with the Drama College environment where there were a lot of people who were intensely emotional and demonstrative.

But that wasn't who Carol was — she was loyal, generous and funny but she was also very private. She had lost her mother at a early age and it felt like she kept people at arm's length so that she couldn't get hurt again. But that's me playing at being an amateur psychologist.

Anyway, Carol took a year out to become full-time Student Union President at Central, so she ended up graduating the year after I did. She went to work at the Birmingham Rep in the Education department and then eventually went home to Scotland. She settled in Glasgow, where she worked for TAG theatre.

Carol supported me through all my ups and downs. When I was miserable in Plymouth, she sent me tacky postcards of London and countdown calendars to make the time pass quicker. She read at our wedding. She took me to the theatre during the times when I wasn't being creative at all. She didn't judge the fact that I wasn't involved in Drama in any way. Well, not overtly anyway. I knew that she was disappointed that I wasn't working in that world — she felt I had the talent. But she didn't say it out loud. Like me, she wasn't into confrontation. She just exuded her disappointment. Sometimes, it was like having another family member — your biggest fan yet able to make you feel guilty for not achieving your potential!

She was very pleased that I did the Edinburgh Festival and came through on the train to watch the show. But then, of course, I went back to my office work — what a let down!

Even when we lived miles apart, we kept in touch constantly. For years we'd talk every Saturday night. Then we moved to email and spoke on the phone less frequently, usually in a drunken state.

She'd started Internet Dating but wasn't having a lot of luck meeting anyone special. She talked about David a lot though. He had been a potential love interest but when they met, they found they were better as friends. Looking back, that was probably her decision. We met him at Karen and Steve's wedding in 2002. He was lovely. And Carol was really happy. She seemed settled and content. I knew she and David weren't a couple but they were good together — at whatever level. It was a great day.

Four days later Carol was found dead at her home in Glasgow. She hadn't turned up for work that day despite being due to hear about a promotion and hadn't called in to explain. Her colleagues were worried and the Police ended up breaking into her flat. It was a blood clot. Apparently, she wouldn't have felt anything.

After she died, I was devastated. But it made me re-assess my own life hugely. By now I was working in another office, having been made redundant from Blick. And I was totally miserable. It wasn't enough for me in any respect. At that point I knew I was truly living the wrong life. I wasn't even writing through my misery. I was just stagnating.

But a few months after Carol's death I saw an advert for a Drama teaching job in Wantage — the town where I lived. It was like Fate had stepped in. I applied and got the job. It was a temporary contract which could get extended. I would start in October 2002. It was very daunting, going back to teaching. To be honest, I was terrified. But it felt like the right thing to do and I knew Carol would be proud. She had always set herself goals and achieved them; mostly surpassed them actually. She made things happen. I needed to be more consistently like that.

It was the right decision. After the initial terror had subsided and I'd settled in, I really enjoyed the teaching. It was hard work and the students were not at all easy. But I loved the variety of teaching from Year 7 through to the Sixth Form. My tutor group were hard going to start with, especially as I took them for English and Drama as well as delivering their pastoral care element — we spent a lot of time together. But after all the 'testing' that always occurs, we mostly got on really well. They were a lovely bunch of kids. They sent 'Get Well' cards to Todd and kept in touch with me for ages. But I never got to see them again after he died and everything went tits up.

I think Carol would have been proud that she had something to do with getting me on the right track again. I hope so anyway.

Subject: brace yourself, it's a long one!
Send: Sun, 18 Jul 2004 05:11:36 +0000

i know, i know, ive been useless about keeping in touch recently!

where were we last time? i was off to meet the crazy canadians for a trip to the cinema wasn't i? we didnt end up going to the huge place just stayed local. then we met up the next day for more of the same! the cabaret was good. some of it was excellent...some less so!

after adelaide i travelled back to melbourne and stayed with bev and phil again, in their lovely flat. i explored melbourne a bit more on one of the days and then went on a trip to phillip island on the other day. i saw the fairy penguin parade, which i'd decided i wanted to do when i was planning my trip. it was worth it! they are the smallest penguins in the world and each day they come in from the sea and return to their burrows in the sand dunes at dusk. they are quite cautious as they come in...the beach is v big when you are that small! so they wait til there is a group and then march up together. they are very noisy considering their size!

after another mammoth train journey i arrived back in sydney and decided to chill out for a few days...no more travelling round for a bit! i still managed to visit the cinema frequently however. (a new cinema has opened at bondi junction...dangerously close!) i think ive seen most of the films on general release now! and i met the canadian girls again before they returned home. i also saw a play at the opera house and did a tour of the building. its an amazing building, in an amazing location...cliched, but true!

i also took a cruise around the harbour this week. it took up most of the afternoon and we had dolphins swimming alongside the boat.

yesterday i met up with my writer friend michaeley and explored her area of town. in the evening we saw bjorn again performing a free concert at darling harbour on a floating stage. michaeley and i wore fluffy, flashing bunny ears and had our photos taken...havent checked the paper yet..hehe. fame at last!! after the concert we met up with my friend doro (from the ayers rock trip) and her friend max. the 4 of us went to a great malaysian restaurant. then went on to kings cross with the intention of dancing the night away. but it wasnt to be! the clubs were far too serious. i just wanted to dance to some trashy disco stuff!! ho hum!

today ive packed my bags again, as im due to catch a train to brisbane in a while. its another mammoth journey..14 hours this time. i arrive at 6.30 in the morning. im sure i'll be totally boggled by then! i have a couple of days in brisbane, then im off to fraser island, then onto byron bay. i get back in 2 weeks and then have to start thinking about coming home!

how time flies!
speak soon

lots of love
kate xxx
ps. thank you for all the cards. george and fay are very jealous!

We're All Going On A Summer Holiday

Todd and I hadn't had a proper holiday since our honeymoon in 1995. We'd had weekends away and stayed with family lots. We'd even had a few days in Jackie and Ken's caravan. But no actual holiday together that involved getting on a plane and staying in a hotel. I'd been lucky in that I'd won a holiday to Lanzarote in 1999, but Todd hadn't been able to go with me because of work, so I'd gone with Sarah instead.

In 2002, we managed to get away for two weeks in Corfu. It was early in the season as neither of us liked it too hot and it meant it would be quieter too. We stayed on the outskirts of a little place called Paleokastritsa and we had a balcony and a view right out to sea from our room. It was all pretty basic but we were happy. It was a chance to be together, to relax.

We explored lots in our little hire car and found out of the way restaurants where you saw the fish going from the boat to the kitchen — where you could choose which one you were going to eat.

We lay in the sun, we read books, we listened to music. We had a holiday. It was a new experience.

We started planning our next trip soon after we came back. In 2003, we'd be off to Bulgaria...but that never happened.

Monday 8th September 2003

Go into Bude. Walk loads along the beaches and through the town. Todd is really energised by his blood transfusion. I forget to take his sunglasses and a drink. I feel guilty as he needs both. We have a drink at a beach café and people watch. It's like old times.

We try to catch the bus back to Stratton, but none turn up. We sit on a wall for ages. We eventually get a cab back to the B & B.

We have supper in the local pub. Todd has excellent scallops. Again, like old times.

Tuesday 9th September 2003

We wander around Stratton and spot a few things to buy for Christmas presents. We return to Bude and have a wander around the museum and shops. We have fish and chips for lunch. A bigger lunch is better than a big supper for Todd as he gets less hungry as the day progresses. He develops a passion for maple and pecan Danish pastries from one particular bakery. I buy a king size duvet as it's a bargain(!) then we get the bus back to Stratton. We return to the pub where Todd has a cheese and tomato doorstep sandwich for his supper.

Wednesday 10th September 2003

Todd gets up early again and wanders around Stratton before I'm even awake. He window-shops and buys cigarettes. After breakfast, which he eats plenty of, we get the bus to Bude where he buys some bait, then we get a cab to Widemouth Bay. Todd sets up his fishing rod on the shoreline and I sit on his tiny fishing stool and read my book. The stool keeps sinking in the very wet sand and we have to keep moving inland as the tide is coming in fairly fast. He doesn't catch a thing, but loves the opportunity to do something normal, something he's always loved. He insists on carrying a huge holdall with his fishing gear in it. It weighs a ton because of all the weights he decided to bring. He looks like he will get a booter at many times during the day, but avoids it, until the inevitable happens and his foot disappears into a deep puddle. Booter!
We get a cab back to the hotel. Sarah arrives. We go to the pub again for supper. Todd has a cheese and tomato sandwich again. Before this time, he was a creature of habit too – if they were on a menu, he'd always have mussels followed by calves' liver.
Throughout these few days his pain relief has remained static and he's not needed top-up Oramorph. His awful, smelly burps are in evidence (they always were) – a mixture of his illness and the cocktail of drugs he takes lead to a very sulphurous burp experience. Kim is always convinced that Todd's been eating lots of eggs!

Diary; 4pm sick
5pm POO AGH

Thursday 11th September 2003

My 33rd birthday.

Todd has managed to get me a silver and diamond ring. He's never done anything like that before. It's rather emotional. He's only managed to get it with the help of Mummy and Sarah. Mummy had got it from Paddy and Libby (stall-holders who had supplied most of my jewellery collection) and posted it to Sarah who brought it to Stratton with her. I wear it every day for over a year.

We go to the Eden Project for the day. We try to make Todd take it easy by insisting he travels on the land train rather than walking all the time. He insists he'll be fine but we make him. He doesn't stand a chance with both of us bugging him! We get glared at by the pensioners who are also queuing.

You see, Todd didn't really look that ill. He was very thin, but at first glance you wouldn't think anything was amiss, just that he needed to eat some more pies. We had a great time wandering around the biomes and even managed to find a statue for me to copy.

Afterwards we drove to Port Isaac and had a bit of a walk around and then drove along the coastal road for a while before returning to the B&B. We went to the pub for supper again (more cheese and tomato sandwiches), but returned to our room early as Todd's pain was returning. Not surprising really as he'd done so much that day. Kim arrived that evening and I ended up sharing Sarah's room as the boys had an early start the next day.

Diary; Oramorph 120mg @ 10.45pm

Friday 12th September 2003

Todd and Kim left early to go on a sea fishing trip. They left from Padstow and everyone on board was sick as it was rough out at sea. They came back with a few fish and full of stories. Todd was pleased as, for once, he wasn't the only person throwing up.

Sarah and I drove down to Marazion and St Ives for the day. We spent lots of time sitting on rocks, thinking.

Saturday 13th September 2003

Kim's birthday.

We'd bought him a few Harley Davidson gifts as he had become obsessed with getting a big motorbike. Penny wasn't so keen, but he was very determined. He did end up getting his bike – not a Harley though.

Kim drove us back to Wantage. We had to go via Axbridge so Todd and Kim went in Kim's car and I travelled in Sarah's Beetle for that part of the journey.

After Axbridge, I joined the boys. Dido's 'No Angel' CD was playing in the car and I found it very hard to listen to. I tried not to get upset and failed. At least I was on the back seat and out of view.

Sunday 14th September 2003

The day of the KCC triathlon. Todd had organised this challenge in the past – kayaking, cycling and running, in and around Abingdon. It took a lot of organising.
This year he didn't attend.

Lee and Julie visited and we went to the Lamb for Sunday lunch. Todd ate a roast dinner and even managed pudding. Another good day.

It wasn't meant to be like this. We worked so hard to make it work between us. We were both determined to have a successful marriage because our parents had all divorced. It wasn't perfect, nothing is. It was hard work. But it was meant to be forever. Until we were old people. Leaning on each other and moaning, like old people seem to do.

We finally seemed to be getting to a good place. At last, I was happy with work. Todd was content with his job. He loved his social life. We had a really nice home. It took us so long to be able to get a house (albeit a rented one) and have enough room for all our things. Our wedding presents weren't unpacked until five years after our marriage began. Life seemed better than it had been for a long time. We'd had a difficult time, but had mostly put it behind us. Things were definitely looking up. And then this.

I have no trust in good things happening again now. I really don't believe in a happy outcome.
I don't see the point of anything.

I still have some of Todd's liquid morphine. It would be enough. And quick. I'd just stop breathing and go to sleep. It would take the pain away. It's a painkiller. The ultimate painkiller.

But what if I couldn't find him?

Hold It

Sarah and I discovered the joys of statue photographs on our first visit to Dublin. We saw a sculpture of two women gossiping on a bench and felt that I could join in too.

This carried on over the years. I'd do it whenever I could – in London, in Cornwall and in Morecambe. Todd discovered the fun of it when we were in Corfu. There were loads of statues there and we copied or participated with them in plenty of places. I particularly like Todd as Achilles with an arrow in his heel (a cocktail decoration I believe!)

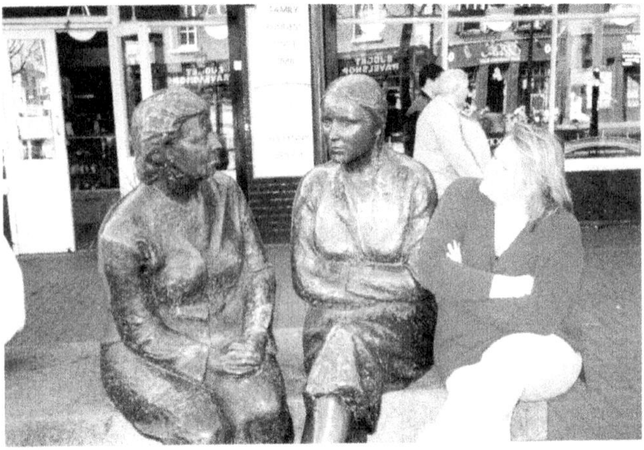

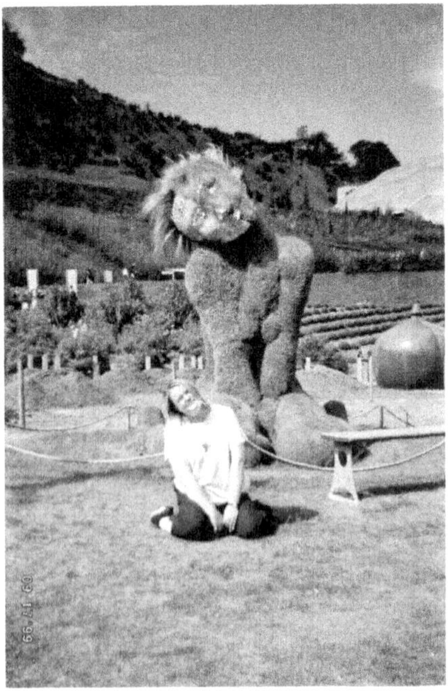

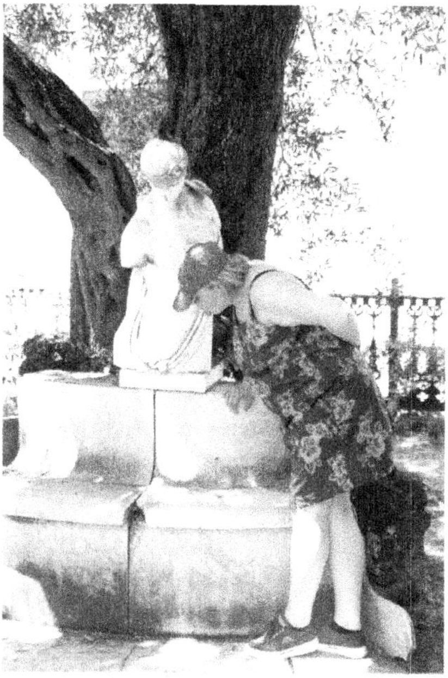

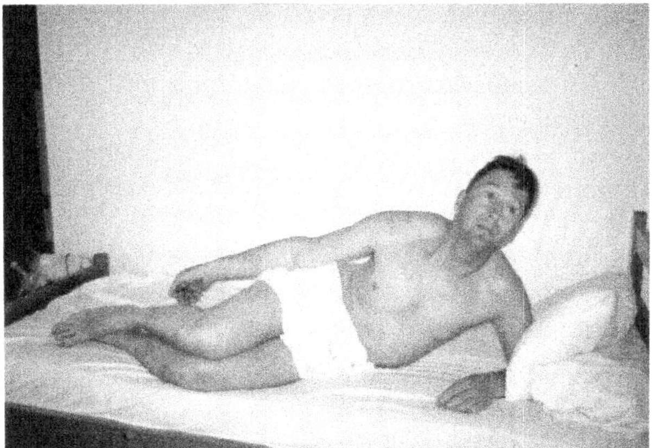

Steak and Kidney

Ingredients

5lb Diced Stewing Steak
1½lb Diced Ox Kidney
5 large Onions, diced
4 oz Beef Dripping
8 – 12 oz Tomato Puree
Water

Method

Brown the onions in the dripping.
Add the beef. Fry gently for ½ to ¾ of an hour, stirring every 10 minutes (season with black pepper and salt when the meat is sealed all over).
Add the kidney and cook for another 15 minutes.
Add the tomato puree and cook for 10 minutes stirring well.
Cover the meat with water and simmer until cooked (about 1½ hours)
This can be done on the stove, as unlike thickening with flour, you have very little chance of catching

This pie mix can be topped with a variety of pastries, some of which will be covered later in this book (Todd didn't get as far as the pastry section)

Scaramouche. Scaramouche. Shall We Do The Fandango?

Summer 2002; The Queen's Golden Jubilee. We were invited to Kevin and Panda's celebration party. It was all rather tongue in cheek — a garden party where red, white and blue had to be worn. Everyone bought into it and looked pretty amazing. Todd was a bit cooler than the average attendee however, he had blue jeans, red hoody and white FCUK t-shirt on. His nipple piercing was evident through it...

Being a musician, lots of Kevin's guests were musical too. And very serious about it all. As the day progressed, there were performances in various locations. At one point, everyone congregated in the lounge and were encouraged to play the instruments that were there. Todd took up a cello and started to play it like a violin and then like a guitar. There were a few shocked faces. I think the non-musicians were meant to stick to the percussion instruments — or just watch! But Todd was always naughty. He liked to stir things up.

So, it was hardly a surprise that later on, when we were in the garden, he started an impromptu rendition of Bohemian

Rhapsody. Well, he had got fed-up of the traditional rounds that were being sung by the 'choir'. So, he just launched into, 'Mama, I just killed a man'. To start with, it wasn't noticed, he was in competition with quite a few choristers. But gradually, they started dropping away and listened. He went from beginning to end, complete with guitar solo, without stopping (He was accompanied, weakly, by Sarah and myself initially. We soon gave up though as we realised we were rubbish and that he certainly didn't need our help). When he finished there was a bit of a shocked silence and then applause.
He later got asked if he was involved with any choirs. He just gave them a look that said 'no' he wasn't. Nor would he be.

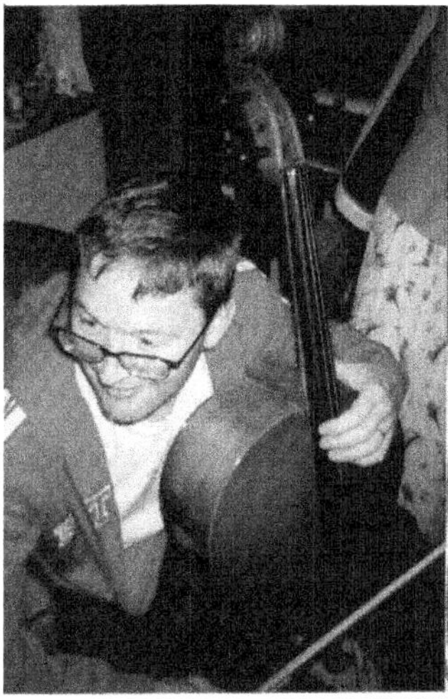
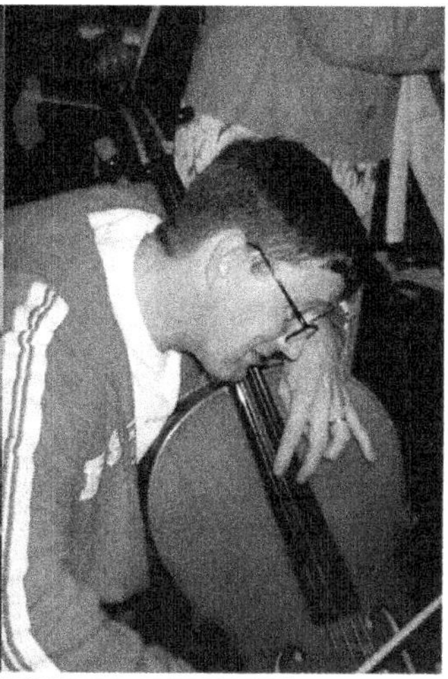
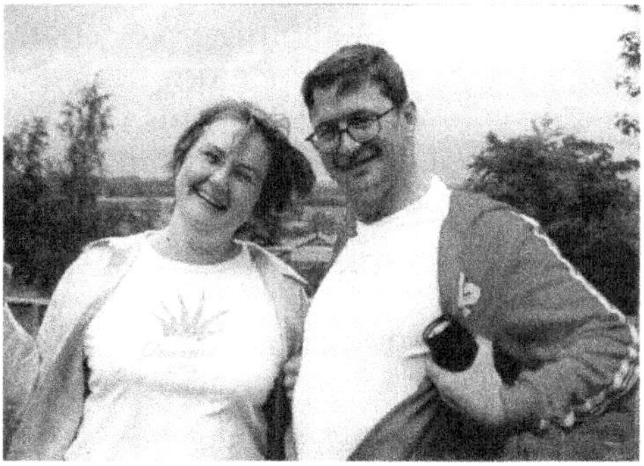

Monday 15th September 2003

7am tummy bug? Todd thinks he has some gastro bug as he is throwing up and has diarrhoea.

GP notes that Todd has vomiting symptoms x2 this morning. Some abdominal cramps. Has been fine for 2-3 weeks. Feels hot. Has vomited his tablets this am. Advised to take Oramorph in place of vomited tabs. Drink only water. Gastro enteritis? Obstruction?

GP return visit. Patient's condition the same. Vomited again. Tired.

GP return visit. Patient's condition improved somewhat. Nausea less and no vomiting past couple of hours. Has been slightly feverish all day. No medication needed since am tablets. Examination of patient; temp 37, pulse 88 BP 124/84. Abdo generally tender, without rebound. Bowel sounds v active.

All points to gastro-ent rather than recurrent obstruction.

Continue clear fluids only and rest. Call if symptoms deteriorate, as should be steadily improving now.

Anne, from Todd's work, due to visit but had to be cancelled.

Tuesday 16th September 2003

10am blood test
11am appointment with oncology consultant
12.30 chemo
3.30pm Oramorph 180mg
Consultant's letter; attends for start of cycle 3 of chemotherapy. (blood) counts satisfactory therefore proceed as planned. CT of thorax, abdomen and pelvis requested as per protocol. He plans to go on holiday between the end of the 3rd cycle and start of the 4th and we will need to schedule his treatment accordingly.

We'd decided that our Bude holiday had gone so well that we would go away again. John and Pat had offered to pay again –this time for a cruise. I'd been trying to get reasonable quotes for insurance and was finding it really hard. Some companies were quoting amounts that were in the thousands.

Wednesday 17th September 2003

Dr Shackleton; patient's condition improved yesterday. Was given chemo as blood count OK. Weak but vomiting settled. Some abdo pain yesterday. Generally, on the mend.

Thursday 18th September 2003

Diary; 1.40am Oramorph 120mg

Friday 19th September 2003

Diary; 8.45pm sick

Saturday 20th September 2003

Dr Shackleton; vomiting over last 48 hours. Anti-sickness injection given 11am, but worn off by evening. Another given 11pm
Diary; sickness all day
Oramorph 120mg @ 5am

Sunday 21st September 2003

5.12am call doctor, continually being sick
7am doctor arrives, injection given.
12.26 call doctor, on chemo, ongoing sickness
2pm doctor visits. Injection. Ambulance booked
16.28 call doctor. Ambulance not arrived.
Ambulance control contacted by doctors as no response to 3 queries.
Ambulance collects patient.
Admitted to Blenheim Ward, Churchill Hospital, Oxford.
Consultant's letter; Mr Morris was admitted with uncontrollable vomiting following his first cycle of Gemcitabine and Capecitabine. He was unable to keep any food down and was pale and

dehydrated. He was noticed to have lost a significant amount of weight since his chemotherapy and was tachycardic and generally very unwell. His abdomen was generally tender, distended, but soft with a 3cm liver edge.

He was treated with IV fluids and a syringe driver of Diamorphine for his abdominal pain with some anti-emetics added and some steroids and the Capecitabine tablets were stopped. His abdominal pain settled, but his vomiting was difficult to control. A CT was therefore performed which showed some distal small bowel obstruction which is probably due to adhesions. It also demonstrated progression of his liver disease and he was therefore discussed with Professor Friend. Prof Friend agreed to transfer him to the John Radcliffe for assessment of a palliative procedure to relieve his vomiting and obstruction and enable Mr Morris to go home.

We had extensive discussions with Mr Morris and particularly with his wife about his poor prognosis and the fact that the chemotherapy had had no effect on his disease. We discussed the fact that he would not be well enough for further chemotherapy but would arrange to see him in clinic and assess him after his discharge from the John Radcliffe.

My diary - Saturday 6th December 11pm

Todd died two months ago.

It's A Family Affair

Todd loved his family. He didn't see lots of them, but they were very dear to him. He was especially close to his grandparents. Nan and Gramps lived in Brislington in Bristol and they had been together forever. They argued constantly but were inseparable. When we arrived at their house (usually unexpectedly) they'd be delighted to see Todd but would have to run through the list of grandchildren until they got the right name. Luckily there were only 4 to choose from; Kim, Todd, Lee, Scott. But apparently, whichever of the boys turned up, the same thing happened.

We'd sit in their back room and have our separate boys and girls conversations. Todd would tell me afterwards that his chats with his grandfather were always about his ill-health. Gramps would go into great detail and more often than not he'd show Todd the catheter bag strapped to his leg.

But they never stopped bickering. That role seems to have been taken over by Kim and Penny now. Todd was devastated when Nan and Gramps died.

He was also hugely upset when his step-father Ken died in 1993. Like me, his parents had divorced when he was young, but his mum had re-married. Ken was a very down-to-earth bloke who made Jackie really happy. He also had a family of his own that Todd got on with pretty well for many years. Until things went a bit tits-up after Ken's death. That got partially resolved when Todd was ill, but not totally. Todd became close to Ken over the years and was understandably very upset when he died.

He became closer to his dad when John was diagnosed with leukaemia. Times like that make a family pull closer and that's exactly what happened. John had very intensive treatments so understood what Todd was going through when he had chemo. Luckily John's leukaemia went into remission. As time passed with John's health improving, he and Pat would go on regular holidays. They'd discovered a zest for life — it was there to be lived. There was no point in waiting to do things, why not do them now? They became really hard to get to see as they were so often away. Life carried on we were all busy. And Todd didn't keep in touch very well. He would sporadically get calls from Kim telling him to phone his dad or his mum. He was a boy — he was rubbish at keeping in touch!

He was close to his mum obviously but she, like his dad, was often busy with sewing or friends or keep fit or her theatre group. She always had lots of news to pass on when he did eventually call.

His relationship with his brother, Kim, was also close. Apparently, they'd fought like cat and dog when they were younger, but as adults they were pretty similar. I first met Kim when he returned from a year in Australia with his then girlfriend, now wife, Penny. Todd and Kim would meet up when time allowed. Kim was more of a grown-up as the years passed. He had children and even got a caravan. His two boys were Sam and Harry (middle name Todd) and my Todd loved them dearly. As with my nieces and nephew, he proved himself to be very good with children. However, he did like to give them back at the end of the day.

He was also close to his cousins, Lee and Scott and they'd often come to our parties over the years.

Of course, all these relationships changed after Todd was diagnosed. Each of the family members reacted differently to the news and struggled to comprehend Todd's illness in their own ways.

Subject: some koalas, some waves & lots of sand
Send: Tue, 27 Jul 2004 05:21:47 +0000

hi everyone

well, the journey to brisbane was horrible!! they turned the lights off at 9.30pm and we were meant to sleep from then on. surprise, surprise i couldnt!! i arrived in brisbane like a zombie at 6.30am. luckily my hotel let me check in really early so i could sleep for a while and get a shower. once id revived a bit i wandered round brisbane and proceeded to get extremely lost! i walked miles in the wrong direction...i think i must have been thinking i was a boy because i didnt stop to get any directions!!! eventually i ended up on the south bank...the arty area. i had a wander round and sat on the man made beach that they have there. i even found a cinema, where i saw stepford wives. i know...its unlike me to watch movies! in the evening i had a fantastic italian meal and rolled back to bed.

on the next day i went to the lone pine koala sanctuary (watch out for amusing post!) and managed to cuddle a koala. thats another thing id wanted to do before i came over too! id even printed off a voucher on the internet whilst i was still in wantage, which entitled me to a free g'day pack! (a poster and guide book!) i also hand fed kangaroos and listened to talks on different creatures. and because it was a weekday, there werent too many people around.

after that i travelled up to hervey bay on the tilt train and set off on my fraser island trip. fraser island is the largest sand island in the world. there is no soil nor any rocks there at all. just a sand base and some tenacious plantlife. the island is covered in rainforest too. the only

way to travel is in a 4 wheel drive vehicle as the roads are just sets of bumps! its a good job i dont get travel sick anymore! i wasnt sure about it to start with. i wondered what was so special about a big sand pit! but george and fay had insisted it was one of the best places they had visited in australia so i went along. im so glad i did. it was amazing. there are really clear lakes and huge sand dunes and wonderful rainforest walks.
one of my highlights was swimming in champagne pools. its a small semi-sheltered pool right by the surf. the waves crash over the rim and foam up..like champagne bubbles. and you get swept away by the force of the water! im not describing it very well, but it was truly amazing!

we stayed in the wilderness lodge...a world-renowned eco-resort, in dorms. i was with 3 young english girls who were fun. there was a cool bar called the dingo bar where we did drinking and dancing!

the trip lasted for 3 days and we saw a lot of the island. i even went up in a tiny aeroplane and saw it from above.

once back in hervey bay, i met up with the girls again and a few of the others from the trip. we ate chinese food and went to an irish bar...very aussie!! some of us ended up on the beach at 1.30am listening to the waves and watching shooting stars.

the next day i went on a whale watching trip. hervey bay is famous for being an excellent whale spotting destination. we saw a few...it is still early in the season. but the ones we did see were amazing. they are huge! and very noisy! we had a pair of them taking it in turns to breach...spectacular! then they started slapping their tail fins on the water which was v dramatic. i met up with the chaps again in the evening.

then yesterday was spent travelling again. i had cab, bus, train, coach, coach and minibus! i arrived at my hostel in byron bay and was shown to my room by the lake. its called an island retreat and basically its a permanent tent with a proper bed in it. its really cool. its right by the lake and is very private. last night there was a massive rainstorm and i just lay there listening to the water cascading down the canvas whilst i was all cosy inside. i slept better than i had in ages! this morning i had a bush turkey walking across my deck, closely followed by a huge lizard!

the hostel is called the arts factory and its very funky. there was a fire twirling workshop this morning...i thought id better not...id end up setting fire to myself by mistake probably!! i might go to the midnight movie though. and tomorrow im probably going to the day spa for a treat! i also want to go on a sunrise walk whilst im here. byron bay is the most easterly point in australia and gets the first sunrise of the country's day.

so im off to go for a welcome walk now and to work out where everything is.
speak soon

lots of love
kate
xxx

Flat Out

Ironing? What's that about? We used to own an iron and ironing board when we lived in Weston but it only got used when I needed a blouse for work or Todd needed a shirt for an interview or a night out. But mostly we wore clothes that didn't need ironing.

It was just too dull

I found that if I hung the wet washing carefully a lot of creases fell out. And those that didn't — who cared? Not Todd and certainly not me. I don't even own an iron or ironing board now. Life is just too short!

Having chosen an outfit for Todd to be wearing in the coffin I presented the funeral directors with a bag of un-ironed clothes and explained why. When he came back 'prepared,' the clothes had been ironed, so the funeral director (the lovely Linda) went around him and scrunched up his clothes so they looked crumpled!

Wednesday 24th September 2003

GP; spoke with staff on Blenheim ward. Todd in for few days at least. Vomiting improved with sub cut pump. Needing increasingly hi dose analgesia. Still on IV.

Friday 26th September 2003

I'm meant to be going to Mummy's in Axbridge for a couple of days on Todd's insistence that I needed some time away. This was arranged prior to this latest hospital admission and is therefore cancelled.

Sunday 28th September 2003

Todd discharged from Churchill hospital – to go to JR instead for possible surgery.
Consultant's letter; ...he was transferred from Blenheim Ward to the surgical ward at the John Radcliffe Hospital with a diagnosis of small bowel obstruction. This was managed conservatively and no operative procedure was required. He was transferred back to the palliative care team.

Todd due to go fishing. Trip cancelled.

My diary - Wednesday 1pm

I'm finding it very hard to care about Christmas. It seems to be the subject on everyone's lips. Normally it would be for me too. I'm not sending cards at all. I don't mind giving presents to family (being Mrs Organised, I had them ages ago), but I can't play at happy families.

So many people say I must not be alone on Christmas Day. But it should be my decision. I've been so powerless for months now and by making the decision for me, my family are taking away any power I might have now.

I really don't know what I want to do, but I know that I can't pretend that everything's OK. I'm definitely not going away though, which is a relief.

I'm not sure if the Prozac is working yet. I know I have an upset stomach (as predicted). Last night my pupils were really dilated and I felt a bit hyper – like I was on Speed. I felt I was gabbling on the phone to Karen and Sarah. I hope that doesn't continue.

I had to have blood tests this morning. It was really icy and I fell over on the way to the surgery. I felt foolish and sore. As usual, it took ages to find a vein and I was very wound up. I feel so wet when I can't cope with blood tests. Todd had to have so many and never complained. Even when his veins started to collapse and they couldn't get a needle in. I can't help it though. I've always been rubbish with needles.

I went into school yesterday to observe a bit – and get a feeling of school again. The Sixth Formers were lovely, gave me a big group hug. They are putting on Trojan Women on Thursday night. I might try to go – I'll decide on the day.

Then I called in to Knapps, the funeral directors. They had sent me a message label to fill in and put on their Christmas tree. It was a really nice idea. I chatted to Linda for a while. I don't know how anyone can work as a funeral director – such a difficult job. She said that people think they are hard hearted but that's not the case at all. Of course they get upset. I know Carl did at Todd's funeral. Quite a few people told me that.

Squeak Squeak

In 2002, during one of my short trips to Cornwall with Sarah I kept getting text messages from Todd saying 'squeak squeak'. I asked what he was on about but he wasn't very forthcoming. I returned home none the wiser.

As I opened the front door I could see straight through the hall and lounge to the patio doors. And through them was a hutch.........containing two guinea pigs. They were instantly christened Bubble and Squeak (the only names available to guinea pigs I believe!) they were very little and very scared. I gave them a cuddle and cooed over them. They didn't stay little for very long. They became huge big boys. They never stopped eating. They got on well together and occasionally would pretend to be gay and a do a bit of dry humping of each other. It passed the time I suppose.

That was just the beginning though. A couple of months later we were asked to take in a rabbit who was about to lose her home. Apparently, the people couldn't keep her and if they couldn't find a home, they were going to set her free in the wild...

We agreed to take her in. She was very pretty and was just 8 months old. Todd re-named her Dylan after the character in The Magic Roundabout because she would flop herself out in the lounge whenever we let her in. She seemed very chilled out and also pretty friendly. She'd come and say hello when we sat on the floor in front of the settees and would let you stroke her.

But I'd been reading about rabbits (I always had to be fully informed about things — I'd read all about guinea pigs too. I'd even read cat behaviour books when we used to have next door's cat visiting us). I'd found out that they liked company and it wasn't really fair to keep one on its own. Next time we were in Swindon at the multiplex we popped into Pets at Home and saw a gorgeous brown ball of fur with lop ears — like Dylan. He was a male and he was gorgeous, but we didn't get him as we were off to the movies and the shop was closed when we came out. Dougal (we'd already named him — a bad sign!) prayed on our minds though and later that week we returned and got him — along with another hutch. We knew we couldn't put the two of them together as they were both complete and we didn't want baby bunnies. So, we scheduled to have both of them 'done' and then gradually introduced them. They fell in love and became inseparable. Even though they'd been neutered, Dougal still seemed to have lustful feelings; he just didn't know what to do with them. Dylan couldn't help him out, she didn't have a clue either. When he started bonking her head, she just let him get on with it!

They used to spend time outside where the hutches were and indoors with us. They were very entertaining — often better than the TV. But you had to watch the cables. Bunnies love electrical cables for some odd reason. Ours were often found with nibble marks before they were interrupted. Dougal managed to chew through 2 telephone wires, once when I was on the phone to Mummy. She didn't notice I'd gone for some time — she just kept talking!

By now, the back garden was looking rather messy with 3 hutches and a run. So, Todd decided to build 'Bunny Mansions' to house them all. This was a huge structure, well over six feet tall. It had three floors, then cupboards in the pitched roof. There was storage underneath for the dried food containers and a ramp to allow the rabbits to get in and out. Bubble and Squeak had the ground floor flat and Dylan and Dougal had the maisonette above, with a ramp between the two floors. It took ages to build but was amazing. They loved it, although it was often quite tricky getting them to go to bed at night. We'd have to chase them round the garden and herd them up the ramp. And often you'd get one in and turn your attention to the other, just to find that the first one in had decided to come out again. They thought they were hugely amusing

On another visit to the pet shop, we spotted a white albino rabbit. We were told that she was a female and was bigger than the others as she was older. We decided to have her. There was plenty of room in Bunny Mansions and another girl shouldn't cause a problem. But we put her in her own hutch initially, just until she'd made friends with the others and been neutered too.
She went to the vets shortly afterwards to be done, and they proceeded with the op. However, they discovered, on the operating table, that she was actually a he. A very immature he. And the reason s/he was bigger was that he was just a bigger breed. So, he came home – neutered almost twice over and felt a bit sorry for himself. He was named Zebedee (see what we did there?!). Unfortunately,

he never got on with Dylan and Dougal. Each time they met, there would be a huge fight and a white rabbit with blood on it is a horrible sight. So, he always had to be let out on his own. He was more of a placid boy; he had albino red eyes and wonderful soft fur. But he grew. And grew. He was a huge bugger. He'd lie stretched out in the lounge and you couldn't believe how long he was. He liked to eat odd stuff too — mostly the back of the settee we discovered. He was also a cable fan. He managed to chew through the cable of the Dyson whilst Sarah was hoovering. He just looked a bit shocked apparently and went and had a quiet sit down.

The animals were very popular with all our visitors and we loved having them. Looking after them was the only reason I got out of bed on the days following Todd's death.

When I went to Australia, I had to find a temporary home for them all. Dylan, Dougal, Bubble and Squeak went to stay with Gen and Kate and their children, Thomas and Anna in Wroughton, whilst Zeb went to friends of theirs in the same village. Zeb got on really well with the little boy in his new family and they would lie stretched out together. He ended up staying with his new family and even got a girlfriend called Florence!

Bunny Mansions moved to Axbridge once I returned to the UK and then came to Cornwall too. Sadly, the bunnies both died around New Year of 2006 but Bubble and Squeak still chunter away, although they are old geezers now. They get lots of attention from passers-by in their new home, in Cornwall.

(Sadly, at the time of writing, Squeak had just died. He is buried in the garden. Bubble died soon after Squeak...he was buried next to his pal)

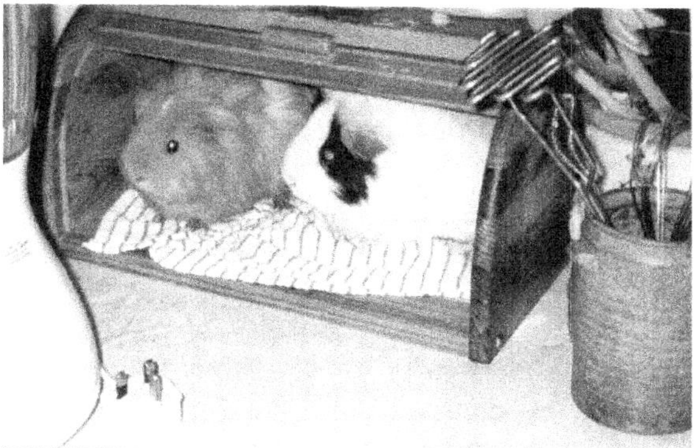

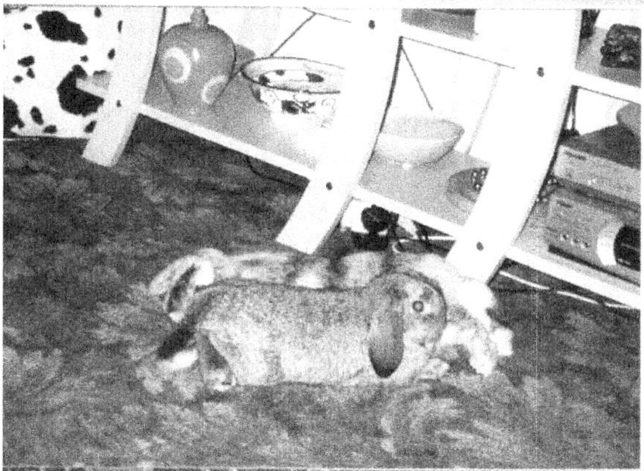

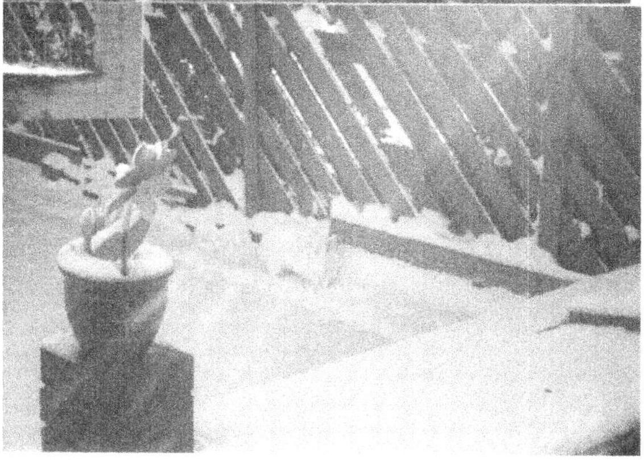

Monday 29th September 2003

Palliative care team letter; Todd and Kate had a number of conversations with oncologists, surgeons and nurse specialists acknowledging how seriously unwell Todd was, and facing the potential of him having a prognosis of days to weeks.

An abdominal x-ray demonstrated resolution of the partial bowel obstruction seen a week earlier, together with faecal loading. Todd's constipation was managed using increased doses of Codanthramer and various enemas. Todd was keen to get home as soon as he could and I understand through his wife Kate that they would like him to die at home if at all possible.

Todd is fairly sleepy at present and there may be room for reduction of the dose of his Diamorphine. If he remains free of nausea, there may be a role to reduce or remove the Methotrimeprazine from the syringe-driver. Todd does not measure his daily Codanthramer doses. However, he does vary his dosage according to his degree of constipation. In discussion with Dr Minton it was suggested that Todd could take up to 60 or 80 mls daily provided this was helpful. Should his stools become hardened and pellet like the addition of Movicol sachets could be considered provided that Todd can manage the high fluid intake required. Further involvement of acute services can be assessed as Todd's needs dictate.

My diary - Thursday 1.30am

I can't sleep again. And it's too late to take a sleeping pill now.

I need Todd so much. I just don't know how to be without him. I'm so scared of everything.

I can't stop thinking about going back to school. I don't really think I can do it. I just feel I ought to. I don't feel I ever want to do anything ever again to be honest. Just stay here in the house where it's safe.

I feel so detached from everything. It all seems unimportant. Insignificant.

I wish he was here now. Or I was there. Wherever that is.

Best End of Lamb, with a Dijon mustard and herb crust

Ingredients

1 French trimmed best end of Lamb
2 tbs coarse grain Dijon mustard
4 tbs fresh bread crumbs
1tsp Herb de Provence

Method

Cross cut the fat on the lamb and rub over the mustard.
Mix bread crumbs and herbs, season well and sprinkle over the mustard to a depth of about ¼ of an inch.
Roast in a hot oven for about 25-30 minutes.
Serve with Julee.

Thursday 2nd October 2003

Todd discharged to return home. He has an intravenous pump delivering his Morphine and anti-sickness drugs.

My diary - Saturday 5.30pm

The pills seem to be 'working'. I don't like how I feel at all. Like I said before, it's like being on Speed. I know I sound 'bright' but it's not how I feel. I'm gabbling when I talk to other people. I popped to Sainsbury's earlier and felt very anxious again – first time for a while.

I hope these side effects die down – I can't carry on like this. It feels very unnatural.

I'm going to Sarah's tomorrow. It's a long journey. I hope it goes OK – it's when things go wrong that I feel unable to cope.

I'm going because it would have been Todd's birthday on Tuesday. He would have been 41. Except he won't be. He'll be forever 40.

My diary - Tuesday 16th December

Todd's birthday

Subject: chill out time

Send: Mon, 02 Aug 2004 03:57:38 +0000

hi everyone

well, i didnt manage to go on the sunrise walk...i never managed to get up early enough.....oops! i just found the whole time really relaxing and gave in! i visited the lounge cinema twice...its fab, you can lie down and watch movies. it was very comfy and also a real bargain. i also visited the main byron cinema a few times...for comparative purposes obviously!

the beaches in byron were great...incredibly soft, fine sand and not too busy. and yes of course i got some silly tan lines again!

i also found some funky shops to indulge my retail addictions! byron was a bit like glastonbury, but warmer and by the sea. but there was the same mix of hippies and arty types.

and on my last day there i went to the day spa and had some fantastic treatments...a sauna, a scrub, a wrap, a massage and a facial. i was totally blissed out by the end...barely able to move!

i undid the good work of the masseur on saturday, as i had a 15 hour journey back to sydney! yesterday, i re-visited the rocks market in the city and then met george and fay in coogee to watch the sun set. then we went for a great italian seafood meal.

today, im organising to send back my excess luggage. i seem to have more stuff than i arrived with! tomorrow, i am going to get a travel pass and go wherever the fancy takes me! then in the evening i am going for a thai meal with george and fay before i head back home on wednesday evening.

i cant believe that it is almost time to come home again!

lots of love
kate
xxx

Friday 3rd October 2003

11.30am nurse visits. Patient's condition worsened. Out of hospital and significantly worse than before. Has lost lots of weight. Ankles markedly swollen (secondary protein lack) pain controlled currently and no nausea. Diarrhoea ++ so stop Co-Danthramer. Consider dropping Diamorphine to 300/24 hrs.
Advised to moisturise his feet. Getting v cracked. (secondary rapid onset oedema)

OEDEMA; **an accumulation of fluid in the tissue. Oedema of the ankles is quite common, if movement is restricted. This swelling is usually 'dependent', meaning that the pressure of fluid in the legs, from prolonged standing or sitting, pushes it into the surrounding tissues. It is also caused when the intake of protein into the body is inadequate.**

1pm Occupational Therapists visit to evaluate house and Todd's needs. Will provide 'feet' for the settee, so that it's not so low to sit down on. Also, a commode and a fleecy cover for the settee to be more comfortable to sit on.
Talk about getting a bed in the lounge. Todd agrees it might be an idea but is happy with just the settee (he has always slept on it during the afternoons for years)
Thomas visits (he has now returned from working in Libya)

Dad and Pat visit.
Oramorph taken, but no record of the amount in Todd's diary this time.

Todd and I try to sleep together in our bed. He finds it impossible to get comfortable and returns to the settee. The stairs are a huge trial now and after this he doesn't go upstairs again.

My diary - Saturday 4pm

I just took down all the sympathy cards. I felt it was time that they weren't there anymore. There were 115 cards and letters in all. I re-read them all. My eyes are very sore now. Of course, I shall keep them. I don't seem to be able to write much at the moment. So much is happening – I feel like I'm getting on a runaway train again. Why do I never feel in control?

Lemon Torte

Ingredients

3 pints Whipping Cream
12 Eggs
10 oz Caster Sugar
2 x 8" Sponges
1 pint Fresh Lemon Juice
12 leafs of Gelatine
Zest from 4 lemons, finely chopped

Method

It is very important to fully prep this recipe before starting to make it.
Line four 8" sponge tins with a double layer of grease proof paper.
Cut the sponges in half to make 4 thin sponges, and place them in the bottom of the sponge tins.
Soak the gelatine in the lemon juice.
Separate the eggs and put half the sugar with the yolks and half with the whites.
Gently warm the lemon juice to dissolve the gelatine.
Whip the egg yolks and sugar to sabayon stage.
Whisk the egg whites to ¾ peak.
This is best done with 2 machines making the sabayon in a food processor, while whisking the egg white and then the cream.
Once you have the three elements whisked up it's time to combine and this is best done by hand.
Making sure the lemon juice is cool to the touch, place all four preparations in a large bowl and fold together

lifting the lemon juice from the bottom of the bowl until you have a smooth texture.
Divide the mixture into the cake tins, sprinkle over the lemon zest and place in a fridge for 4 hours.
After 4 hours, remove the tortes from the tins and keep in the fridge until required.
(Do not leave in the tins for more than 4 hours, as the lemon juice will start to attack the tins and discolouration will appear around the torte)
These tortes freeze very well.

Saturday 4th October 2003

8.45am 150mg Oramorph
11am district nurse visits. Re-do the IV pump. He needed quite a lot of Oramorph yesterday. Was due to reduce to 300mg Diamorphine in pump. Suggest stay at 320 today. If still needing a lot of Oramorph call for advice again.
11.45am 150mg Oramorph
Midday Roger and Athene visit
12.04 district nurse calls doctor. Todd has sore mouth, possibly thrush. Prescription faxed.
12.30 Sarah arrives
1pm 150mg Oramorph
3pm Mummy and Kevin visit
4.25pm doctor visits. Increase Morphine in syringe driver.
10.05pm doctor called as Todd had collapsed.
11.45pm doctor arrives.

Todd refuses ambulance. He had collapsed – weak legs, hit head on stairs. No vomiting or other change. No bleeding. Requested check over, back on settee now. Fall tonight – not concerned. He is very weak. Chat with carers. Clearly approaching the end, patient really not in discomfort, but v weak.

Easter Biscuits

Ingredients

15 oz Butter
3 fl oz Lemon Juice
1 lb 2 oz Caster Sugar
3 Eggs
2 lb Plain Flour
1 lb Currants
8 – 10 Drops Cassia Oil

Method

Cream the butter and sugar
Add the eggs and lemon juice
Add the flour, the oil and the currants.
Roll out to ¼ - ½ and inch and cut out 4" rounds.
Bake on a greased tray at 180C until golden brown

Sunday 5th October

Sarah still staying. We take it in turns to sit with Todd 24/7. Feel he can't be left alone after the fall.
He's still really lucid. Drinking lots of lemonade, but not eating now. Still smoking – although inside now, rather than in the deckchair by the patio door. House stinks of weed. Covers the smell of the stinky burps!
Lee visits
Then Scott and Rachel, and Lee and Julie visit too. Todd sleeps through most of the visit. Sarah goes out so there aren't so many people there all at once, hoping that maybe others will follow her lead. They don't. People don't realise.

Brandy Snap Baskets

Ingredients

8 oz Golden Syrup
8 oz Granulated Sugar
8 oz Butter
8 oz Plain Flour
½ tsp Ground Ginger

Method

Melt the butter, sugar and golden syrup over a low heat.
Then add the ginger and flour.
Beat, off the stove, to a smooth paste.
On a large baking sheet (12" x 8" minimum), that has been greased and floured, place two table spoons of the batter, one at each end of the tray and bake at 180C for approx 8-10 minutes.
When you remove them from the oven, the brandy snaps should have spread out to form 5" rounds and most of the bubbles on the surface should have burst.
Leave to cool for about 1 or 2 minutes (you won't get them off the tray if you don't do it then).
Place them over a small cup and leave to cool.
These brandy snaps will keep in an air tight container for 3 – 4 weeks.

Monday 6th October 2003

After staying up through sections of the night with Todd, Sarah leaves to go home. We've been promised a nurse to do the night shift with Todd tonight so we no longer need to do days and nights. She needs to get home.

We run out of clear lemonade. John gets some when he visits.
Kim and Jackie also visit.
11.45am Oramorph 150mg
1.30pm Oramorph 150mg
2.45pm Oramorph 150mg
3.45pm Oramorph 150mg
4.45pm Oramorph 150mg
GP; patient's condition worsened. Retching today with small amounts of dark black blood in vomit. No fresh blood. Pain significantly increased today too. Needing several doses of 150mg Oramorph. Discuss whether patient prefers to stay at home if there is a significant GI (gastro-intestinal) bleed. He would. Increased pump to 400 Diamorphine and 50 Nozinan. Stop oral steroids though I think the bleeding probably comes from the tumour ulcerating into the small bowel.
Examination, pulse rate tachycardia 120bpm, BP reading low 70/50
7.30pm Doctor revisits. Patient's condition worsened. Patient has deteriorated. Remains in pain and v restless. Given Diamorphine 10mg sub cut and syringe driver increased to 500 24hrs and 5mg Haloperidol added. Calmer since Diamorphine.

Doctor revisits. Patient dead. Expected. Called by Kate, wife. Fixed dilated pupils, no resps, no pulse.
Certified dead at 9.15pm
Undertakers called. Collect Todd's body.

Sarah drives back from Lancashire.

My diary - 6th October 2003

After Dr Shackleton's 7.30 visit I realised that this was nearly it. She asked if I wanted her to stay but I didn't. I wanted to be alone with My Boy – just us. She gave me her home number as we both knew I'd need it shortly.

After the doctor left it was suddenly very quiet. Todd wasn't agitated anymore, nor in pain. His breathing had quietened.

I lit candles all around the room and put on some music. It wasn't a sick room anymore, just a peaceful one. He was sitting on the settee and I sat next to him. I put my arm around him and held his hand.

And I told him how amazing he was. How he was loved and cherished by so many people, especially me. How I would always love him.

And then he went.

And he didn't hurt anymore.

Smoked Salmon Terrine

Ingredients

6 lb Smoked Salmon
8 lb White Fish
4 Large Onions
2 ½ lb Butter
¼ pint Brandy
¼ pint Tomato Ketchup
¼ pint Lemon Juice
1 tsp Cayenne Pepper
1 tsp Nutmeg
1 tsp Ground Black Pepper
30 – 40 Gherkins

Method

Poach the white fish and onion in a little water.
Drain and cool.
When cool puree in a blender.
Line four 12" terrine moulds with cling film and then with smoked salmon, hanging the ends of the salmon over the sides of the mould about 2" (this will be folded over when the mould has been filled)
Puree the rest of the salmon.
Cream the butter and add all the ingredients beating well.
Half fill the moulds with the mix and then lay the gherkins down the centre.
Finish filling the moulds, wrap over the smoked salmon and place in the fridge.

Tuesday 7th October 2003

Thomas arrives
GP; death administration. Death certificate issued. All Todd's medical team informed.
Go and register Todd's death in Oxford.
Return medication to chemist.

Pan Fried Quails With An Orange and Raspberry Sauce

Ingredients
8 quails (2 per person)
1 Onion, finely chopped
8 Oranges
6 oz Raspberries
½ pint Demiglas
1 oz Butter

Method
Remove the legs from the quails and peel off the skin, remove the breasts from the carcass, and take off the winglets. Roughly chop the carcass and fry lightly in oil. Add demiglas and simmer for 10 minutes.
Lightly fry the chopped onion for 2 minutes, add the quails. Cook for 5 minutes, turning often.
Add the juice and zest of 6 oranges and reduce by half. Add the demiglas after straining through a sieve. Simmer for 10 minutes then add ¾ of the raspberries and cook for a further 5 minutes.
Arrange on warm plates and garnish with orange segments and the remainder of the raspberries.

Friday 17th October 2003

Todd's funeral.

TODD ANDREW MORRIS
16th December 1962 - 6th October 2003

Order of Service

'Wish You Were Here' by Pink Floyd

Opening Words - Jenny Perry

Tributes - Jenny Perry
Joe Shave
Kim Morris

Extract from 'Dart' by Alice Oswald read by Thomas Duggan

But what I love is midweek between Dartmeet and Newbridge, kayaking down some inaccessible section between rocks and oaks in a valley gorge which walkers can't get at. You're utterly alone, abandoning everything at every instant, yourself in continuous transition twisting down a steep gradient big bony boulders, water squeezing in between them. Sumps and boils and stopper waves. Times when the river goes over a rock, it speeds up, it slaps into the slower water ahead of it and backs up on itself, literally curls over and you get white water sometimes as high as a bus or house. Like last November, the river rose three or four foot in two hours, right into the fields and I drove like mad to get to Newbridge. I could hear this roaring like some horrible revolving cylinder, I was getting into the river, I hadn't warmed up, it was still raining, and the surface looked mad, touchy, ready to slide over, and there was this fence underwater, a wave whacked me into it.

Silence

'Love's Advocate' by Phoebe Hesketh
read by Hermione Gulliford

I remember sitting together in parks
leaning over bridges
counting trout and swans
holding hands under arches
kissing away suns
and moons into darkness

I remember platform good-byes
last-minute trains
slamming us apart
and my non-self walking back alone.
I remember smaller things
a pebble in my shoe
and you throwing a match-box on the Serpentine

I stood still hearing the years
flow over and over
as over a stone
in a river-bed
polishing, cleaning, wearing away.
But I still remember the last day

What I cannot remember is how I felt –
mind, love's advocate,
must remind heart
of the end, the abyss
The bottom of the world remains;
each day climbs to a new start

Committal
'Sail Away' by David Gray

Closing Words - Jenny Perry

'To Boat Or Not To Boat' by William Nealy
read by Roger Wiltshire

To boat or not to boat, that is the question:
Whether 'tis nobler in the mind to suffer the
Cruel jests and loud derision from more
Courageous boaters, or to lay futile braces
Upon vast watery obstacles and by not
Rolling up, there drown. To die, to boat
No more, or by portaging to circumvent
The hydraulics and the myriad pointy rocks
That flesh is heir to; 'tis a consummation
Devoutly to be wish'd. To carry, not boat
For to boat, perchance to flip – ay, there's the rub.

'Bohemian Rhapsody' by Queen

Todd

By Sarah Duggan

Todd loved white water, children and the sea
Todd loved rabbits, guinea pigs and the Grand Prix
Todd loved fishing, cat-napping and fudge
Todd loved wildlife parks, cooking and squash
Todd loved thrills, tortoises and Bob Marley
Todd loved Pink Floyd, bamboo and everything funny
Most of all, Todd loved Kate

Donations to Cancer Research UK
c/o H J Knapp & Sons, 4 Church Street,
Wantage, Oxon. OX12 8BL Tel. 01235 772205

Butterflies and Lights

In the days and weeks after Todd's death I would wish for him to haunt me so I could see him again. Even though the idea of seeing his ghost was slightly scary, it was less scary than never seeing him again.

He never did turn up in ghostly form. But I did feel he was around. I started seeing little lights out of the corner of my eye in the lounge. If I looked directly towards the corner where they seemed to be there was nothing there. Yet, from time to time I could see them with my peripheral vision. Somehow, I knew it was him. I knew he didn't have a body any longer and was coming back as pure energy.

I also started seeing Red Admiral butterflies all over the place in the house — despite it being winter by now. Again, I knew it was Todd. I'd talk to the butterflies as if they were him. It probably sounds loopy but that's what I saw at the time. It was comforting whether it was real or not.

Subject: final ramblings from the land of oz
Send: Wed, 04 Aug 2004 08:07:11 +0000

remember what todd used to say at the end of every conversation before this all began? he always said "have fun"......and i've been trying to go along with that during this trip. sometimes that has been easier than other times, which was as i had expected. mostly i have had a fantastic time and certainly dont regret coming over to australia. i have met some fantastic people and seen some amazing sights. some of the things that stick in my mind follow;

ive visited 5 of the 7 states in australia.
ive visited the cities of sydney, melbourne, adelaide, canberra and brisbane.
ive taken trips to the red centre, the great ocean road, kangaroo island, phillip island, fraser island and the blue mountains.
ive met tour guides called les (the first and still the best!), leith, mark and dave (rather too many recreational drugs consumed there methinks!) and many others whose names i dont know. they were an amazing bunch of blokes.....all very knowledgeable and passionate about their country.
ive travelled on big aeroplanes, little aeroplanes, inter-city trains, inter-state trains, tilt trains, city trains, scenic railways, coaches, minibuses, 4wd vehicles, buses, ferries, sea-cats, boats, trams, harleys and camels!!
ive seen over 30 movies (best = the mother, eternal sunshine of the spotless mind and shrek 2! worst = godsend) iive seen over 10 plays and shows (best = mum's the word at the opera house and the berlin cabaret in adelaide....worst = vampirella at the darlinghurst theatre)

ive visited many museums, galleries and wildlife parks, so im now hugely cultured!
in sydney i have visited; bondi; the cbd; kings cross; paddington; darlinghurst; newtown; centennial park; oxford street; taronga; parramatta; coogee; watsons bay; manly; darling harbour; millers point; dawes point; circular quay; milsons point; surry hills; cockle bay wharf and woolloomooloo.

some of my favourite places were; the waterhole at uluru; kings canyon creek; sydney harbour bridge; watsons bay; bondi; my tent in byron bay; the great ocean road; the seals and sea-lions on kangaroo island; st kilda in melbourne; the sound of melbourne; the berlin cabaret in adelaide and glenelg in adelaide.

ive met some fantastic people along the way. like doro, kristin, jenny, felix, tash, michaeley, catherine, heloise, izzy, steve and rob. i hope we can keep in touch and meet again sometime, somewhere.

also, bev and phil....big thanks again for the lovely accommodation...i hope you have that tabard now bev?!!

and, of course, george and fay. they have given me the run of their flat in bondi and im SO grateful to them. it meant i could act like a local sometimes and be a traveller at other times...but with slightly less luggage! i hope you get some lorikeets to frequent your new balcony!! and i also hope that you carry on wearing the pirate eye-patch and moustache george! whilst wearing the wombat watch and reading the wombat book!

finally, some of my favourite moments (i cant include them all, there are far too many!)
* being dared to go in the sea on the south coast and doing it with kristin, jenny, felix and tash.
* watching bjorn again on darling harbour, with

michaeley, whilst wearing flashing pink bunny ears.
* touring sydney on the back of a harley.
* playing in champagne pools on fraser island.
* watching the fairy penguin parade.
* cuddling a koala, called woogy.
* feeling blissful at the buddha spa.
* watching shooting stars and listening to the waves on the beach at hervey bay.
* hand-feeding the lorrikeets on the balcony
* sitting around the campfire on the red centre trip.
* getting the minibus trapped in the sand on the red centre trip (sorry les...it still makes me laugh!)
* watching an afl (aussie football league) match in the rain.....go the swannies!!
* whale watching at hervey bay.
* listening to a rainstorm whilst sleeping under canvas.
* sleeping in a swag.
* going to bed at 4am in a top bunk in a big dormitory and then having to get up at 5.30am to go to kangaroo island.
* twirling round on bondi beach in the dark, with a sparkler in each hand, on my last night in australia.

lots of love to you all
kate
xxxx

ps. the winners of the postcard competition are as follows;

prize for sheer volume of post; my mummy
2nd prize in the category; sarah
3rd prize; john and pat

prize for best memory jerker; sarah's card of morecambe

prize for best interpretation of bad taste card; penny's card of a taste bud

and overall prize goes to my mummy again, with her card of weston-super-mare
circa 1974!

prizes will follow shortly!!

My diary - Wednesday 6th October 2004

It's a year since Todd died. Everything is so vivid from those last few weeks we had together so I've been remembering it all very fully. It's horrible. The good memories are hiding again.

I can't believe a whole year has passed. It still feels really recent, like it just happened. In my head it did – he just slipped away from me again. How many times will I experience this? Todd dying over and over again. And I can never change the outcome.

There is still a real pain within me. Obviously, it's especially acute today. I knew it was going to be hard. Of course, it would be. I just can't believe that so much time has gone by. How did that happen?

It hit me a couple of weeks ago – how fast these months have gone by. It all seems very fuzzy. Australia seems like something I made up, it's only the photos that prove to me that I was there.

I went to Bristol Zoo today – it was one of our favourite days out. The giant tortoises made me smile – I sponsored one for Todd for his birthday once. He loved tortoises and always wanted one. I even went and visited the reptiles and the bugs this time. Before I was too scared. I'm a lot braver these days. What's the worst that can happen? Oh yes – that's happened already.

I spent nearly an hour in the nocturnal house, waiting for quiet between groups of school-children. I went to see the penguin and seal coast twice too. I saw the plaque that I had dedicated to him there, which made me weep. Nothing soppy. Just 'For My Boy'.

I also had a moment in the canteen – not sure why there 'cos the food wasn't lovely and we usually took a picnic anyway. I remember one on my 30th birthday. We had lobster and crab with all sorts of salads. A Todd special!

Then I let rip in the aviary. It was a mixture of laughter and tears, mostly tears. I was alone in there and just remembered us getting caught in the rain in the outside section. And commenting on the birds' funky hairdos.

Back home now. Although it's not really home. It's Mummy's house. Up in my old room watching the clock creep towards 8.30. Giving in to the sobs which have been threatening all day. I knew I needed to be alone today. I'm sure she doesn't really understand why, and I know she wants to help – but how can she? She can't bring him back. And she can't mend my broken heart.

My diary - Wednesday 27th October 2004

I'm in limbo. Totally stuck. It feels like my life has ground to a halt. I can't find a new job. I don't even know what I really want to do. I just know I want my own space. I'm not being the person I want to be at the moment. I'd worked so hard to "not sweat the small stuff", but I'm finding that harder and harder to achieve. The small stuff is taking over and I feel unable to deal with the important things.

Everything is so hard. It seems that I am expected to be 'back to normal' now. But I'm not – nowhere near it. How can I be? My other half is still missing. I still feel empty. I still love Todd.

I just phoned the funeral directors about Todd's ashes. They are still in Wantage. I want to be able to scatter them alone, somewhere special. But I want to drive to do it. And I can't do that until I pass my test. And I can't get my head around driving.

Yet another thing I'm failing at – driving, finding a job (they don't even bother to reply to applications), finding a home, sleeping, starting over, being me. Fail, fail, fail, fail, fail, fail. Christ, I'm pathetic.

Self-pity is so unattractive.

But I can't seem to help myself at the moment. I try so hard to keep positive but nothing feels like it's going right. And my acting reserves are drying up. I think the cracks are showing.

My diary - Monday 15th November 2004

I've been so sensitive over the last few days. Everything sets me off – songs, lines of dialogue, everything.

The latest thing was a passage in a book. A character died, but she left behind a note for her love.

Todd didn't leave a note or a card or a letter. He just went.

He never wanted to acknowledge what was happening to him so he didn't talk about his illness or the fact he was dying. It meant I couldn't either.

He only spoke about it once. It was during his final stay at the Churchill Hospital. He realised he didn't have much longer – a couple of weeks maybe. We were outside in the garden having a ciggie with his drip-stand in attendance. It was quiet – just us. We talked about a lot of things –regrets about not having his child (he forgave me), regrets about his affair (I forgave him – I had done a long time before. I even asked if he wanted me to get in touch with her). He couldn't visualise my future at all – just knew that he wanted me to be happy – an impossible wish really.

Then he asked me to stay with him overnight. But he was in a ward with other people so I thought it wasn't possible. But Joe was coming to collect me so it wasn't possible. But I was making excuses. It should have been possible. I should have stayed to talk to him. I should have stayed. I should have.

It was the ONLY time he talked about the reality and I let him down. Perhaps that's why he didn't leave me a note or a letter or a card.

Because I didn't deserve one. Because I let him down. And I can't forgive myself.

Subject: post script
Send: Mon, 16 Aug 2004 17:59:02 +0000

well i'm back! and it's very very strange!

i forgot to mention how to contact me back in england. for the time being im staying at my mums house in somerset.

please carry on keeping in touch!

lots of love
kate
xx

ps. did you know that kangaroos can swim (it is true kristin and jenny...leaf was correct, unfortunately!!) that there are 600,000 camels in Australia and that the major cause of death for said camels is obesity...who would have guessed that?! (well i know you would doro...but you had insider information!)

did you also know that aussies eat pumpkin and beetroot ALL the time. or that tim tams are the best biscuit ever?

well...you do now!!

My diary - Sunday 30th January 2005

So much has changed and yet so much has stayed the same.

My final application of 2004 was taken up. I had an interview on 1st December and was offered the job. It's for two terms initially – in Penzance. I moved down a month ago. I'm renting a 3-storey house in the town which is gradually getting sorted out. The animals have a new home in the back yard and I constantly hear the yell of seagulls.

School is hard work. I knew it would be. It's been 18 months since I taught properly. The job is part-time Drama and part-time cover work, which is a little odd.

I've had a couple of nights out and I'm gradually meeting people.

Seemingly, I'm making a good new start. I've always wanted to live by the sea in Cornwall and I have a decent salary and a nice house.

So why does it all seem so fucking pointless? I feel totally unsettled. Like I'm just marking time. I'm not fulfilling Todd's wish for me to "be happy". I feel extremely alone. Very far from everyone and everything I know, and I honestly don't think this is what I want. I think I might have made a big mistake.

I've just moved my internal problems to another location. A location that does not feel like home. That doesn't mean I know where home is, I still have no idea. It's just that this doesn't feel like it. Ordinarily this house would be great – it has some problems, but all old houses do. But there's plenty of space, which I've been craving. I have my own possessions around me – also something I've been craving. But at the end of the day, that's just stuff. I never thought I'd think like that.

But I'm thinking more and more of the feeling of relief I had when I locked all my possessions away in storage, before I went travelling. You see, the travelling bug has not left me at all. When I was having no luck finding a job, I was starting to think about going off exploring again. I knew I didn't want to stay at Mummy's. Much as I love her absolutely, us living together was never going to be ideal on a long-term basis. It was really difficult and the dynamics of our relationship changed totally. Anyway, there was no job in sight so I'd started thinking about taking Tom's advice to do the TEFL training so I could teach and travel at the same time.

Then the job came along and I did the sensible thing, of course. But those same desires are still there. There are so many places I want to see. And if I don't do it soon, I wonder if I ever will. Life could become too comfortable and settled again. And I won't have the guts to go on an adventure.

I want to fulfil Todd's wish – for him and for me. And, at this moment in time, I'm very far from doing that. The only time I've been truly content over the last 18 months was when I was travelling. Maybe that's because I was running away – maybe not. But travelling is the only thing in my life that I've done for me, at my own instigation. Everything else has been encouraged by other people because I'd be 'good at it' or it would be 'useful to fall back on' or because 'you love me'. All very good reasons. But travelling had no expectations. It was purely my own. And I want some more of that.

Life is so short and none of us know how long we have. I don't want to end my days with regrets about things I should have done. I want to experience it all. Grab life with both hands, shake it and see what falls out. Not just take the safe path.

June – October 2003

The time of Todd's illness wasn't all doom and gloom at all. We found a hugely black humour which got us through a lot, although the palliative care team didn't always seem to understand our irreverence. They'd sit with their heads to one side, looking sympathetic and occasionally leaning forward to touch our knees, trying to encourage serious, sad conversations. But, often, we didn't want that and would start giggling and sharing private jokes. It was probably a bit rude and immature and I'm sure we looked a bit loop the loop but that was our way of coping.

On Todd's frequent stays in hospital, he'd always try to escape his bed as soon as possible. He'd be anywhere other than on the ward. He'd refuse to wear pyjamas and be a 'patient' unless he really had to. He'd find somewhere he could have a fag – or a spliff – away from all the medical bollocks. Even when he needed a wheelchair, he'd encourage us to whisk him away. The nurses knew what he was like and gave him certain times which he had to be back on the ward for, but mostly let him get on with it.

It was an incredibly hot summer that year and we started sharing Slush Puppies, sucking out all the flavour until all that was left was white ice.

When he was home, we'd go for walks when it cooled down in the evening. Often that wasn't until at least 11pm. But it didn't matter; we didn't have to keep to any timetable. We'd wander slowly around the neighbourhood, disturbing the local ducks as they tried to sleep, causing lots of indignant quacking.

Todd started noticing his environment a lot more than he ever had done in the past. I would discover him standing by the shelves of 'stuff' in the lounge, taking in the details of our possessions. He also took to moving things around a little, to see if I would notice. And I'd often find a bear from the vast, although now not quite so evident, collection on my bedside cabinet. Or on the bathroom sink. To make me smile.

We became somewhat fatalistic. Along with the hot weather came lots of storms. Before this I'd been really scared of thunder and lightning, but now I was seeking it out. We'd sit in our deckchairs under a tree in the garden and watch the electrical storms. Get struck by lightning? Who cared. It couldn't be worse than what was actually happening.

We spent hours holding hands, our only words being "I love you". Those words became everything. They meant; "I'm scared"; "I'll miss you"; "I wish this hadn't happened"; and "I really, really love you. More than anything in the world". All within those three words.

We had good days out at the wildlife park and we had our holiday in Bude which was lovely. Todd got his model aeroplane and even though he crashed it with me, he went on to fly it successfully with Kim and was totally euphoric about the experience.

We saw more of friends and family than we'd ever done before. Todd felt supported and loved. It wasn't all bad. Mostly it was, but not all. And those are the moments I try to recall now rather than the crap stuff.

What Katy Did Next (part 1)

Moved to Cornwall, to Penzance. Almost as far as you can go without falling off. She had always loved Cornwall and wanted to see if the reality lived up to the dream. It did.

Rented an amazing house which was much too expensive but made her happy. She could see the sea from upstairs and her bedroom overlooked the gardens. There was a particularly excellent tree that she could see as she lay in bed. It was very dramatic and sometimes she saw squirrels in it. The house was a party house. It was often full of people after a night out. Or people coming to visit for weekends. Sometimes there were couch surfers – visitors from all over the world. And sometimes it was very quiet. An oasis for her to just be, surrounded by her beautiful things and frequently illuminated by candles. There were lots of photos in the house to remind her of her boy. She found it odd that no-one in her new life had known her boy at all. That they only found out about him from her stories. That was a hard thing about the new life.

Taught Drama at a local school for two terms. It was a temporary contract which enabled her to move to Cornwall and give the dream a go. The contract didn't get extended as a better candidate was appointed on a permanent basis. The school wasn't an easy place to teach. The students were challenging. But after an initially difficult start, she began to really enjoy it there. Her Head of Department was lovely. The staff were welcoming and supportive. They also liked to socialise. And the students grew on her. So, when she didn't get the permanent post, she was gutted. She looked for other Drama teaching jobs locally, but there were none.

Made lots of lovely new friends. Everyone was so welcoming to her. They took her under their wings and introduced her to different people and invited her along when they went out. She soon realised that her alcohol intake would be increasing if she were to stay in Cornwall!

Had fun with boys. After thinking that there would never be another man ever, she slowly realised that some feelings were coming back. Lustful feelings. She wasn't ready to fall in love again (would she ever be?) but she did enjoy having sex with unsuitable men. She enjoyed it very much.

She realised that she really wanted to stay in Cornwall. So, she thought long and hard and decided that the time had come to pursue her long-held dreams of writing and performing for a living. Over time Drama Queen Theatre evolved as an idea, and then became a reality. A one-woman theatre company, performing to students and to adult audiences. She wrote and rehearsed and performed. And loved it. She realised that losing the teaching job had been one of the best things that could have happened to her. She really hoped it would work, but knew it wasn't the end of the world if it didn't. The important thing was to try.

She moved again, into a little fisherman's cottage in Newlyn. Just about a mile away from the party house in Penzance. It was very different to that home, but was amazing in different ways. She could see the sea from her bed and also the guinea pigs. They now lived in the garden that was in front of the house and got lots of attention from people walking past on their way up or down the steep hill that the house was on. She passed her driving test. At the grand old age of 35. It made so much difference to her life. And she knew that her boy would be proud of her.

She got into a whole lot of bother with money. She had never been very good with finances. Despite there being some insurance payouts following Todd's death, she felt as if that was a bit like blood money and it slipped away, travelling in Australia and living somewhere she couldn't really afford when she moved to Cornwall. It all went spectacularly wrong. But she survived that…she was good at surviving!

She took a job at The Acorn Arts Centre in Penzance, running the Box Office. It was the perfect role for her and only ended when things went tits up and the team were made redundant. She missed being the Box Office Bint…she'd enjoyed selling tickets and talking to customers and meeting performers and watching shows and laminating many, many posters for the display boards outside.

Eventually she fell in love again with a funny, kind electrician. They had lots of fun together and laughed a lot. Until they didn't anymore and the relationship broke up. She didn't regret those years though…they were full of happy memories

…….to be continued!

My diary - 10th May 2006

I decided that today would be the day to scatter Todd's ashes. I'd collected him when I'd been to Oxfordshire. I'd always said I wanted to do this once I had passed my driving test. I was performing a new play in Holsworthy in Devon which was pretty close to Widemouth Bay where we'd had our lovely holiday when he was ill.

I went to the school, performed a play about teenage pregnancy and then ran a workshop with the students. All the while knowing what I would be doing next – I never did like to make life easy for myself.

After I'd finished at the school I drove to a deserted Widemouth Bay. I couldn't find the exact place we'd spent time – him fishing and me reading – but it didn't seem to matter.

I climbed over the rocks to where the water was lapping the shore in my jeans and brand-new trainers. I took the surprisingly heavy bamboo urn and undid it to reveal the hemp bag within that held Todd's remains. Instead of scattering his ashes into the air over the sea I gently tipped them into the waves. I knew that ashes have a habit of flying in the face of those scattering them. I thought Todd might decide to play that trick on me as a final parting shot. Instead, his ashes sank down to the sand – and stayed there. And stayed there. I was sobbing by now as I waited whilst the waves did their work and carried him away to sea. Slowly, the ashes started to ebb away as the waves worked over them, until he was finally gone. I continued crying for quite some time.

Eventually I decided I had to leave the spot, and him, and return to the car.

What I hadn't realised as I'd been standing on the rocks was that quite a lot of people had decided to walk their dogs on the beach all of a sudden. And, more importantly, the tide had been coming in. As I'd been standing on slightly elevated rocks I hadn't noticed. I now remembered how the water had kept pushing us back up the beach on our last visit. I was somewhat stranded in my brand-new trainers. However, the tide wasn't fully in and when each wave withdrew there was a tiny gap when a clearer path to the shore became apparent. I stood on the rocks waiting for the magical moment. But as I jumped off, I realised my mistake as a big wave's worth of water swept over my ankles.

And suddenly I wasn't crying anymore, I was laughing. My Boy's parting shot – a double Booter!

Epilogue - well, sort of

How can it be that I'm a happier person since Todd died? That seems horribly wrong. People say he would have wanted me to be happy and I know that's true. He said it himself. But surely not at the expense of losing him?

No, that's wrong. It's not at his expense, not at all. It is because of him. Because until you have felt the deepest sorrow and despair you don't recognise happiness fully. You learn to grasp it with both hands, almost grapple it to the floor. Because you know it is transient, so you want to hold on for as long as possible and revel in those moments. Until the next chance of happiness comes along, when you will jump at whatever opportunity is presenting itself.

Until I knew that sorrow, I expected to be happy, I felt it was a right. Thought I was a happy person. Now I realise I lived a lot of my life on auto-pilot, took many things, and people, for granted. And often didn't come close to happiness. I let opportunities slide past me and didn't pursue my dreams because it was too frightening. I was scared of failing. Scared of looking foolish. Scared of change. So, I minimised my life. I didn't push myself nearly enough. I did well in the life I had - but it wasn't the right life.

But now there isn't anything left to be scared of. The most frightening thing that could happen to me, happened. And I'm still here. I survived.

Now the fear has gone I'm liberated. Failure? If one thing doesn't work, there's always something new to try. Looking foolish? Who cares what I look like in other people's eyes? If they have a problem with the way I live my life, that's their problem, not mine. And fear of change? Change is embraced these days. Who knows what will happen next? That's the exciting part, not knowing. Who knows how long any one of us have? I just know I have to take My Boy's advice and 'have fun'.

Mind you, it has taken a lot of counselling to get to this place in my head!

It seems like grief is a funny thing, except it's far from amusing. It never actually goes away. You just learn to live with it. It's like a little time-bomb attached to your heart. Sometimes it explodes a bit – giving you a reminder of what has been.

A day doesn't go by when I don't think of Todd and usually cry to some extent. I look at his photo all the time, but I'm not sure if I'd recognise him if I saw him on the street or heard his voice on the phone. I know that's a totally irrational feeling. Of course I would. Wouldn't I?

It's just that time is smudging the edges. A lot of our life together is really vivid still but other things are not. And who can I ask about those moments? Only Todd. So, it seems they may be lost forever.

Well, until I find him on that beach, surrounded by rabbits and guinea pigs that is. But, to be honest, his memory was never very good anyway. He won't be able to help. He always lived in the present, not the past. And that's why I'm writing all this down. So that no more can escape from my mind. That it will be captured. Like a photo.

And in the meantime, I have to concentrate on making new memories. Living my life fully. Because, like I said before, there was no point in both of us ceasing to exist when Todd died.

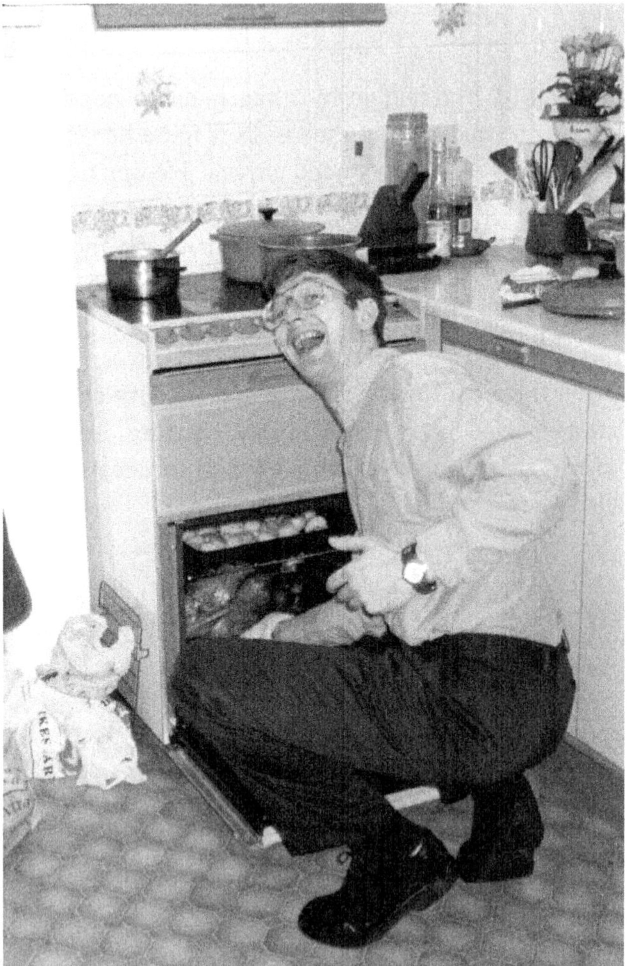

Saturday 21st April 2007

Bamboo 88"

Now

(Ish)

What Katy Did Next (part 2)

After the relationship with the electrician ended, she took up with unsuitable men again. She had always loved interesting adventures! One of these chaps led to a 3-year onny offy kind of a relationship. He was an extremely tall DJ.

She carried on writing and performing. She loved performing her shows in secondary schools but found that budgets dwindled over the years so she did all sorts of jobs to pay the bills alongside the showing off. She also felt that playing teenagers whilst wearing an HRT patch on her arse was pushing the bounds of 'suspension of disbelief' rather too far! During this time, Dullas D'Water arrived...a vintage comedy creation who was a joy to perform. Dullas was terribly filthy but terribly posh, so she got away with a lot. Sometimes she told her personal tales of derring-do and sometimes she acted as a compere for cabaret evenings.

She was lucky enough to perform at the Minack Theatre in Cornwall a few times. Her roles were many and varied, but generally funny. She loved the opportunity to pull faces and make audiences laugh.

Although she was very aware that the audience could be lost in a moment if something exciting happened in the sea behind the stage.

She spent many years as an unhappy part-time barista. But she stuck it out as year-round jobs were rarer than hen's teeth in Cornwall. Afterwards, she vowed never to wear a uniform again.

She began working for her good friend, Stu, as his support worker. Mostly she enjoyed spending time with his guide dog, Austin. And tolerated Stu and his love of cables!

She took a job for one day a week in a gorgeous shop in Penzance called Circa 21. She had to be very careful not to spend all her wages when she was there.

(insert klaxon sound here…or possibly envisage a marching band) She retrained to become an Independent Celebrant. Finally, she felt that she had found her vocation. Firstly, she trained to take funerals – she felt very strongly about the importance of a good funeral. Later, she trained to take weddings, naming ceremonies, re-naming ceremonies, commitment ceremonies. Basically, all the ceremonies from birth through to death.

She got involved with the Death Café movement. Her local group was full of very interesting folks and the conversations were wide-ranging. Obviously, they centred around death, but not in a morbid way. They talked about future planning and what a good funeral might look like.

She was single for quite some time. She hadn't ruled out finding love again but, for now, single was good.

20 years of grief

(sounds like
some sort of
dreary existential
novel
oh, hang on…)

Another Explanation

(I don't think I can call this one a prologue? Hmmm, it's not an epilogue as I haven't finished yet, sorry about that! I think I shall call it a demilogue...)

As you'll have noticed, my writing didn't stop when Todd died. From time to time, I would add to the story. Another memory would reappear, I'd think of something pertinent, etc, etc. But a time did come when I thought I had finished Three More Days. I tried, somewhat half-heartedly, to get it published and had some lovely feedback but no literary agents took it up. I put it away in a metaphorical drawer.

But it kept calling to me, saying that we weren't done. And I realised that the reason it kept being so insistent was that it wasn't actually finished. And nor was the grief. I don't believe it ever will be. That's the thing with grief, you don't 'get over it' – it's there for good. I'm not saying that grief has made me a miserable, weepy mess (although, sometimes, yes) but it has certainly informed the person that I've become.

As a nation, we're a bit rubbish about talking about death, dying and grief. I talk about it a lot! I just want to normalise it really. It doesn't make me morbid. Basically, talking about death won't make it happen any sooner. Promise!

Anyway, I found that I was writing again, especially as all the twenty-year anniversaries were coming up. I felt it was important for me to note how things had changed and how they had stayed the same. How I still thought of Todd often and wished he were by my side. How I imagined our lives might have panned out, if things had been different. How I have been living alongside my grief, doing it my way (bugger, I've given myself an earworm now!)

What follows is a selection of my thoughts/ramblings/witterings from the last few years and especially the time that ran from what should have been Todd's 60th Birthday through to the 20th Anniversary of his death.

Imaginary Children

In the months following Todd's death I would frequently have to explain what had happened to strangers. And I noticed a really strange thing happening. Folks (mostly women folks) would inevitably ask, in hushed tones, whether we had had children. When I answered that, no, we didn't, it had just been us two, I would notice a weird relief pass over them. They would visibly relax and breathe out. "Oh, thank God for that. How awful it would have been for them. What a blessing"

"It was pretty awful for me actually. My imaginary non-existent children coped remarkably well, considering" I didn't reply.

'Coulda, Woulda, Shoulda'

So, what might have been? I've spent a lot of time thinking about this (and trying not to think about this)

1. We followed through on our talks in Corfu in 2002 and started our family. We had two children – a girl (Daisy – always wanted a Daisy) and a boy (maybe a Jacob?). They were welcomed with joy and trepidation (more trepidation from me – remember I'm not a small person expert) But I needn't have been scared as they were both easy babies who grew up to be fabulous toddlers and into wonderful teenagers. We were very proud of them. Daisy was a Daddy's girl who loved sport but was also really clever. She was also very talented at woodwork and used her great-grandfather's tools on occasion. Jacob took after me and was a drama queen from the get go – out-funnying me from an early age. Like his dad, he had dyslexia but, it not being the 60s/70s anymore, he was given lots of help and coping mechanisms. Also like his dad, he was very intelligent, he just needed different ways to express it.

    I took time off to be a full-time mum. And Todd took extended time off too. (Did I mention that we were suddenly independently wealthy? Oh? No? Well, we were!) This time meant that we could bond as a family. We travelled a lot whilst they were small. Never having a particular plan, just going where the wind took us.

It was idyllic. We were very happy.

2. We had four children; Daisy, Jacob, Tom and Betsy. We couldn't afford to take more than the bare minimum of maternity time off. And with no family nearby, we had to use childcare. Life was chaotic but we managed – juggling here, there and everywhere. Todd and I passed like ships in the night as we took extra jobs to cope with the bills. But we were a tight unit – our family. Fiercely loyal to each other. Until the children turned into teens and began to hate us. And each other. There were a lot of rows and many doors were slammed. It felt exhausting and never-ending.

3. We didn't have children. It turned out that when we eventually got round to trying, we couldn't. We'd left it too late. The success rates swiftly diminishing as the years passed. Even with IVF, Let's not get started on the IVF. The hope. The failure. The injections. The overwhelming hormones. The conversations. The questions. The fake optimism. The failure. The silence.

4. All the above and then we split up. No one to blame, but it had been too much for too long. And once it stopped, we had nothing to say anymore. We were broken by sadness.

5. As 3 & 4, but after Todd left, he fell in love with someone lovely. Very lovely and very fertile. And they went on to have a family. The family we should have had. I tried to be happy for him and her. I tried really hard. It was really difficult. I failed.

6. There's no fertility journey. There's no family. There's just the two of us – as it always had been.

    But we fell out of love with each other. Nothing particularly dramatic happened. We just took each other for granted for a bit too long. Maybe we had our heads turned by other excitements? Maybe not?

    Whatever. We split up. The divorce was unpleasant (I believe they generally are), not because we were fighting over money or property as we didn't have much of the former and none of the latter. Just because it was raking through so much history.

7. We separated and had a dreadful divorce that left us both mentally scarred and unable to trust anyone ever again.

8. I got ill and I died. Todd found love again after a suitable time and was happy. She already had children who soon adored him and they went on to have two more of their own. Their blended family was chaotic but happy. Todd cooked

lovely family meals and the lovely lady (who wasn't me) despaired at how messy he made the kitchen. But she loved him all the same. Todd didn't write a book about us.

I'd take any of these options (especially number 1!) instead of what actually happened.

Where is Home?

I'm not sure I've ever really known. For the longest time I still saw Axbridge as home. But actually, when I was there, I lived like Mummy, a little bit separate. It was home because she was there. Mummy's house was home, wherever I was living. Despite all my time with Todd – home was Chestnut Avenue.

But confusingly, home was also in Highbury Parade, Wallingford Street and Bailey Close cos that's where Todd was. Until he wasn't.

Then there were the homes in Wembley and Swiss Cottage – with the Golden Girls.

Of course, the homes that Sarah has had, that I've loved and felt very at home in.

And, finally, the Cornish homes – Penzance, Newlyn, Pendeen and Penzance again. I've been down here for a long time and I love living here. But, is it home? I don't know.

Maybe home was Mummy? Was Todd? Is Sarah? The rest is just bricks?

Maybe it's more to do with fitting in, which is something I find hard. I mostly feel slightly separate from the world around me.

I can adapt really, really well to fit in (four years at drama college y'know) but still – it's often an act.

I think that's why I so often crave solitude.

I mean, I love doing stuff – theatre, comedy, gigs (all the darkened room things where I don't have to actively do anything – apart from the occasional woop and yay. And I don't have to make eye contact with anyone either)

And I love to hold a party. Fill my home with people and try to make them smile. Make ridiculous cocktails, provide a cheese room, always a room for dancing (often provided by a marvellous friendly DJ). Sometimes a forfeit-filled pass the parcel – unless I am drunk and forget all about it until the next day. Drunk Kate? Yes actually. My own parties are generally the only times I get drunk these days – in my safe place. I end up ricocheting off the walls whilst still procuring cocktails and kicking up my heels.

I often don't really end up actually talking to anyone properly. I just appear with glasses in my hands and ill-advised words of wisdom. Some friends can't cope with drunk Kate, I can see the fear in their eyes as she approaches. Luckily, she doesn't make an appearance very often.

Generally, I'm totally sober. Just full of Diet Coke! I don't often need an alcoholic drink to let my hair down.

I love all of the exciting everything at the time. Then I get overwhelmed and have to be very quiet and still for a while. Often there will be compulsive games of solitaire and freecell and sudoku at that point – old school distraction.

Where are you going with this Kate?

Not a clue Kate…….

Jarvis vs Todd

I've often been late to the party through my life. Not actual parties (although…) Y'know what I mean though, I've never been bang on trend, on fleek (I'm still not really sure what that is nor whether it's still a thing), keeping up with stuff.

So, I was late to the Pulp party. But my adoration of Jarvis Cocker soon knew no bounds – and hasn't abated since.

Anyhoo, one night way back when (1997ish?), in the flat in Weston-super-Mare a friend was perusing our CD collection which was varied to say the least – it being largely populated with monthly deliveries from Britannia (remember them?!) to which Todd had a subscription and mostly forgot to cancel the parcels. So, we had all sorts.

I digress, said friend had discovered Different Class within the CD collection and popped it on. I was instantly in love with the sound. And the lyrics. Oh, the grubby lyrics, I loved them! Especially delivered in that Sheffield accent by Jarvis.

I had that CD on repeat on my Walkman for a very long time. More CDs followed and my love affair increased.

Why are you mentioning this, Kate? I'll tell you why! My Todd had a certain resemblance to My Jarvis. Both tall, skinny, geeky, dark-haired and often sporting glasses.

On one occasion we were at a Pulp gig in Sherwood Forest (it was part of their forest tour of the We Love Life Album. I also saw that tour at the Eden Project – the very first Eden session. It was amazing and I fell in love with the place and the band even more – even if Sarah and me did have to buy cagouls in Truro as it was a pissy-downy rainy kind of a night)

Back to Sherwood Pines. This was the big specs period for both the men in my life(!) Before the gig started, whilst it was still light, Todd was getting lots of people doing double-takes. Clearly thinking that Jarvis was having a little pre-show amble through the crowd. It made us giggle. That's all really.

But, yes, generally – tall, skinny, geeky, dark-haired, specs-wearing fellas are still what I'm drawn to. Especially the glasses. I'm definitely drawn to chaps who see me in some sort of soft focus!

Raptors

"Raptors" was a frequent cry from Todd whilst driving, as he spotted a bird of prey soaring above. Hovering or diving. He was very drawn to them and I'm sure he knew all their individual names. No Kate, don't be facetious and add in names like Graham, Lizzie and Bernard at this point! No! Names like eagles and buzzards and bustards! He knew a lot of stuff, did Todd. But I didn't learn them from him...I just learnt to shout "Raptor" whenever one was spotted. Still do.

Going back to the Oak House

There were so many memories wrapped up in revisiting the Oak House. Obviously, it's where I met Todd and fell in love. But it has meaning for just about everyone in the family. Mummy was the bar manager there – in the days of long, brown skirts (with comfy slippers hidden underneath), wine bottles with candles in and hams smoking over the fire. Not to mention the many coins embedded in some sort of resin in the bar itself. It was the 70s after all…

Then Sarah worked there as a teenager. She did Sweets and Starters and then also ran the wine bar in a bonkers way.

Anyway, I was over the moon to be invited to Gen and Tess' wedding which was being held at the Oak. On the night before the nuptials there was a meal for the guests. I've been there quite a few times over the years but this time I had much more of a look around, including the kitchen.

Overall, the place has changed massively – No coins in the bar! No hams! No long, brown skirts! But the kitchen was very similar. Most importantly the walk-in fridge was still there. The place where it all began!

Not so Joiny-Inny

I've never been one for joiny-inny activities. Not one for 'hobbies and interests' and the things I do like to do are often in a darkened room with a bunch of strangers watching something…that sounds filthy! I mean, I love a bit of filth but, on this occasion, that isn't what I meant. I like theatre, comedy, films, musicals (well, some musicals, a lot leave me cold) All things you can do whilst having a nice sit down, in the dark. I often like to read, often lying down. Not necessarily in the dark.

But I've never been one for sports (shudder). I was never very sporty at school, always last to be picked for a team. My PE teacher once chose me to represent our house on sports day in the shotput competition. I'd never done it before but I was chunky and strong-looking (?!) so I was in. Suffice to say, our house didn't win any prizes in shotput that day!

So, I've never been drawn to hockey or tennis or aquarobics or zumba or squash. I couldn't even ride a bike properly (too scared to take my hands off the handlebars, so I could never turn right!) And I was scared that I would drown if I went kayaking with Todd. The thought of the obligatory Eskimo roll filled me with fear.

In a complete departure from my ordinary sedentary enjoyments, I did do a sponsored swim for Diabetes UK a few years ago. The challenge was to swim the equivalent of the Channel, 22 miles, over a period of three months. I can't say I enjoyed it, because I didn't. Mostly I only carried on because people had sponsored me and I didn't want to let them down! That was obviously a blip!

I wanted to be good at everything from the start, so if that didn't look likely, I didn't even try.

Todd, however, would try anything and throw himself right in. And he got good because of that. Todd was a joiner-inner.

My only joining in was with the freaky, geeky theatre gang – that was my tribe.

My Coping Mechanisms
(please note that mostly I just muddled through)

Let it happen! Don't try to bury your head as grief won't go away, it'll just come back to bite you on the arse at a later date. It's hideous but it's natural. The price you pay for love and all that.

Talk. I've chosen to talk to counsellors a lot over the years as they are skilled in listening and let you get on with washing your brain without trying to make it better. Personally, I felt that my relationships with family and friends would alter forever if I spoke my messy thoughts over and over to them. Certainly not everyone is like this and often, for them, friends and family are best. You know me, I didn't want to be a bother.

Write. Letting your messy thoughts run freely on a page is such a release.

Be aware of your own head. This one is ongoing for me. Nowadays, I'm a lot more level than I have been in the past, a combination of anti-depressants and awareness have led me here. It took a long time to realise that I'd probably always suffered with depression and that it wasn't just triggered by Todd's illness and death. I now know that I will follow a pattern of sinking lower and lower. And that it's not until I reach that extraordinarily low point that I will start to climb out again.

I'm sure life would have been/would be easier if I asked for help more often. This is still a work in progress for me. Again, I don't want to be a bother.

Try not the sweat the small stuff (for me, this worked temporarily but I found it impossible to keep up in the long term!)

Try not to feel guilty that; you laughed, you smiled, you didn't think of them every moment of every day, that you got rid of some of their stuff, that you moved house, that you travelled without them, that you started a new life – lots of new lives actually. That you fell in love again. That you fell in lust again (a lot!), that life carried on.

However, I have guilt running through me like a stick of rock, so sometimes (often) I'm not so very successful at this guiltlessness mullarkey…

I'm Not…

An expert

The same as anyone else

That different from anyone else

I just know that I've lived alongside grief for a very long time. Sometimes its presence is very small – teeny tiny in fact. A lot of folks like to imagine this 'sometimes' is more like 'always' all these years later.

For me, it's not. Because some days that grief has the power to completely knock me off my feet. It confronts me with long-buried images or intrusive thoughts fill my head. And I'm back there, in 2003, with a man who is Todd, but not the Todd I want to remember – this is the ill Todd, the dying Todd.

So, yeh, that happens. And I feel I have to be honest about that.

But mostly, I see my photos of him daily and I smile. I talk to him a bit, I think of him often, I am very grateful I had him.

I'm not grateful for what happened, that would be really odd. But I am glad that, because of him, and what happened, I have managed to carry on. It's been a hellishly bumpy road (I think it always would have been; I seem to attract drama) but I'm still here. I still try to live by his conversational fullstop. Have Fun!

5646 Days

That's how long we were together.

21st April 1988 – 6th October 2003

I measured how long that time equated to afterwards as well. I had a feeling the time was approaching but didn't look too closely until long afterwards. Because I would have made a thing of that day...a day that had no real significance. It was just another day without.

7th October 2003 – 23rd March 2019

It's even longer now. (That's how time works Kate!)

The Year of the Plague (and a little bit before)

As I approached the big 5 0, I decided to do 50 things for 50 years and wrote a blog about it. I was 50 in 2020...things didn't go quite according to plan!

What's this all about then? (2nd November 2019)

Hello, it's Kate here. I'm not sure who will want to read my ramblings as I head towards 50 but here I am anyway!

I've had a bit of a mad idea and I think if I write about it, I am more likely to succeed in doing it. The idea is to celebrate the route towards the big 5 0 rather than be terrified and grumpy about it! I've known rather too many people who haven't been lucky enough to make it this far so I'm sort of doing it for them too.

'So, Kate what is this idea?' I hear you ask. Well, imaginary pal, let me tell you...

Over the full year of 2020 I will endeavour to complete a list of 50 things. This is not a bucket list kind of thing. It will be much more achievable! No trips to Antarctica or Fiji in this list (as much as I would love to visit both!) I plan to revisit favourite books, films and places but also do things I've never done before, like skinny dipping! Most of the things I can do alone, some need company and some may need a little help to achieve. I just want it to be a series of lovely things to mark a big day. The big day is in September by the way.

I will share the list shortly...eeek!

The First Ten! (10th November 2019)

1. Go skinny dipping...I never have.

2. Do my own dance-athon...not for charity, just for the joy of it.

3. Watch live performances...I love a show, we know this. I would like to see more.

4. Revisit favourite films...I adore movies. I can do this alone obviously, but if you fancy joining me, please do. Bring popcorn! They will include but are not limited to; Bladerunner; The Rocky Horror Picture Show; Amelie; Eternal Sunshine of the Spotless Mind; Trainspotting and One Flew Over The Cuckoo's Nest.

5. Go and visit animals...animals make me happy, that is all.

6. Get a literary agent/get published...please could 2020 be the year this happens?!

7. Return some generosity.

8. Go to London twice…because I like a visit to the big smoke from time to time.

9. Spend my birthday in Bath…not in the bath.

10. Throw a Penzance party…the usual kind of thing; drinking; dancing; debauchery!

The Second Ten (18th November 2019)

11. See friends from across the years…as many as possible, so get your diaries at the ready chums!

12. Have some naughty adventures.

13. Revisit favourite books…I know Cold Comfort Farm will be in there, along with some other loveliness.

14. Skip along the prom…just because! Come and join me if you fancy?

15. Perform lots

16. Trot every day…I often trot, it makes me smile. It makes other people smile. Win win. After all, this whole 50 things thing is to do happy-making stuff.

17. Walk to Mousehole with Sarah, by the water, in a brave way…we did it years ago in a rather hysterical way. And we scared a dog walker emerging onto the pavement on our tummies!

18. Do lots of kissing…what can I say, I love to kiss!

19. Throw a pot...I think I may well be rubbish at it but I'd like to give it a go.

20. Try new recipes...like a lot of folks, I tend to stick to things I know how to cook. Time to expand my repertoire somewhat I feel.

The Third Ten (23rd November 2019)

21. See more comedy…what could be more happy-making than snortling and guffawing?

22. See more live music…my musical tastes are wide-ranging so this could lead anywhere!

23. Visit galleries and museums…bit of culture innit?!

24. Try some sporty type things, failing that, walk as much as possible …I've been wondering about yoga, pilates, running (although my crappy knees might not be so keen on that idea)

25. Construct a website for Dullas D'Water…she will like that.

26. Taste new things.

27. Get a new hairdo…probably not a mohawk or a mullet though.

28. Print off photos and put into albums…I love looking at my photos and revisiting the memories they contain. Looking at snaps on my phone just isn't the same.

29. Be kind to folks. And to myself...I think I'm quite good at being kind to others, myself less so. As this 50 things thing is as much about my mental health as it is about happy-making stuff, this is kinda important.

30. Visit 5 cities...given my finances, this could be five trips to Truro!

The Penultimate Ten (1st December 2019)

31. Visit five counties…more achievable than five countries.

32. Get the KAPOW tattoo…I've wanted a third tat for a long time. I got the other two in Australia in 2004. It's been a while! I also have an idea for a fourth but let's not get carried away Kate!

33. Fix the doorbell…someone stole my bell quite some time ago. As in years. I really ought to do something about it!

34. Sort all the stuff…I have a lot of belongings. I love most of them. But some things really need to go. I have started this already…trips to the tip, the charity shops and giveaway sites have benefitted thus far. I know I'm meant to be doing all the things during 2020 but I thought that whilst my messy head let me do some sorting, I would run with it. Not literally run obviously…I'm not a total loon!

35. Learn a dance…an actual proper dance with proper steps. Not my usual freestyle kind of thing. This will probably be a thing that I find quite difficult.

36. Sew a frock…a very simple one probably. With a lot of help. It may well end up looking suspiciously like a wonky cushion cover!

37. Be a life model…another naked thing. Quite a few came up when I asked for suggestions. What does that say about me, I wonder?!!

38. Write (and receive?) more letters and cards…I love a text or an online chat, but getting actual mail is a smashing thing. Let's get penning missives! If you would like to join in let me know and we can be pen-pals!

39. Write more of my never-ending novel…this is a project that's been going on forever. Surely, I can find a few hours in 2020 to write some more?

40. See the sunrise.

The Final Ten (7ᵗʰ December 2019)

41. Do a cartwheel...I used to be able to do beautiful cartwheels. In my head I still can. Let's see if I am totally deluded on that score. Somewhere with a soft landing needed!

42. Give a stranger a bunch of flowers.

43. Grow something...I have broken my 2020 rule on this one in a necessary kind of a way. I have weeded and dug over and added masses of compost to the one tiny bed I have by my front steps. I have planted bulbs and am optimistic for spring smiles induced by flowers. There will be crocuses, tulips and aliums. Plus, some mystery ones that may or may not be daffs.

44. Write a children's story...something different to try.

45. Visit Ventongimps...I often drive past a turning for this place, near Truro but have never visited it. Even though it makes me snicker every time I go past the turning in a fnarr kind of a way.

46. Explore my town...I've lived here for years but there are whole areas that I don't know in Penzance. Like most people, I always follow the same routes to places. Time to get lost!

47. Walk some of the South West Coastal Path

48. Entertain more...I enjoy welcoming folks to my home so I shall do it more. I also very much like my own company so I shall enjoy that too.

49. Throw a tea party...always fun to pop on a pinny and do some baking.

50. Start 2020 by doing the Jubilee Pool New Year's Day Dip...the local Art Deco lido is very beautiful. On this occasion I may not be appreciating the surroundings so much! This one actually scares me a great deal but I think it will be a really positive way to start my year of 50 things for 50 years.

Number 50...tick! (1st January 2020)

So, today my 50 things for 50 years started in earnest with a very chilly dip in Jubilee Pool. I'm usually very slow getting into water and thought I'd be the same today. Until I slipped on a slippy bit of pool bottom (!) and made a speedier entrance!

I had a fab gang of pals joining me and a fab one taking snaps too. We even got on the local news!

Considering I was so scared about doing this, I was happily surprised by how great I felt afterwards. Those endorphin chappies are a bit marvellous!

What a great way to start the year...may it be smashingly wonderful for us all!

  ps. I have also completed Day 1 of a years-worth of trotting!

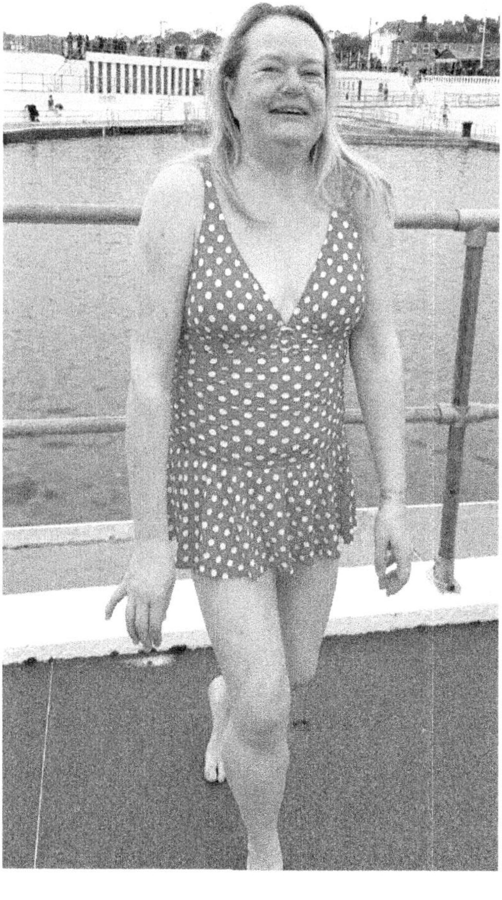

Thinkings...this one gets a bit serious! (17th January 2020)

So, January is difficult, isn't it? I find Christmas is lovely but also really hard, especially since losing my mummy who loved it so.

Then January comes along, all the shiny lights disappear and it just feels...dark.

Clearly my mood is rather low!

I'm still doing little bits of the 50 things...I've seen friends, re-watched Amelie (still love it, did big grinning throughout and great to introduce it to pals) and visited a city. Well, Truro. But it still counts. And I'm finding daily trotting is easier with company. I keep forgetting and have had to do pre-midnight sitting or lying down trotting. That isn't a euphemism by the way!

Anyways, I've been thinking a lot about some of the gorgeous folks I've been lucky enough to have known who didn't get to make their own trot towards 50. I said I was doing this mad, happy-making challenge on their behalf too so I thought I'd write a bit about each of them.

Firstly, Keri. She died late in 2019 of Motor Neurone Disease which came on horribly and rapidly. She was 48. Keri was the most positive, warm, talented and creative woman you could hope to meet. She had a head full of magic. For her, things from the list that are outdoors, in water, creative and smiley.

Next, Emma. She died in the Autumn of 2019. She was 49. I'd only known her for a very little while and wanted much more time to get to know her better. She was hilarious. We had most excellent chatterings online. And when I was low, she offered assistance and a kindly listening ear. Little did I know that she was really battling her own demons. For her, the things include anything daft, so skipping along the prom, doing a cartwheel and, especially, trotting every day.

Next my lovely husband Todd. He died in 2003 of pancreatic cancer. He was 40. What can I say about him? He was my first love. I met him when I was 17 and he was 25. We had many adventures together. He used to roller skate along Weston prom whilst juggling. He cycled, he kayaked, he played squash and badminton. He was a top chef. He made me laugh and he made the BEST Beef Wellington! For him, things that involve being active, seeing animals, trying new foodie things. And getting my book about him, and us, published.

And finally, Carol. She died of an aneurysm in 2002. She was 30 (or 31 maybe, my memory is failing me on this one). I met Carol at drama college in 1990. And she was a fabulous friend. She was very talented, very ambitious, very loyal and very, very Scottish! She would have achieved so much if she'd lived longer. When I was struggling in my first job in Plymouth, she sent me weekly postcards of London as she knew I missed it. We spoke every week too. For her, things that are performance related and to do with letter writing and keeping friendships alive.

So, there you have it. A group of wonderful folks who I have been very lucky to know. I wish we had had more time (I reckon they do too!) But I'm lucky I had any time with them at all.

50 things for me. And for them.

Now I'm off to trot to the kitchen...the stairs will be tricky!

Bits and Bobs (1st February 2020)

I've reached another county. I'm in Devon! Dartmouth to be precise. With my gorgeous sister Sarah. She is my happy place.

In other news I have been doing bits and bobs of my 50 things. I've been catching up with pals (many more to come I hope) And I'm realising that that may be the most important thing I do during this 50th year. I know some stunners (autocorrect wanted to change that to stoners...also apt if I'm honest!)

I've visited a couple of places, tried a new food and caught up with some favourites on the telly box...a slow start, but what do you expect from January?!

I've also started writing a diary. I was given it by my lovely friend Michelle with an inscription encouraging me to write down something super every day so I will have a whole year of positivity to look back on in the future. It's a fabulous idea and, so far, I've done it. Some days I find bags to write about. Other days are harder and I comment on a nice supper or the happiness I get from watching a murder mystery set in sunnier climes.

Today I can write heaps. About Sarah. The sunshine. Sitting in Bayards Cove watching the Hauleys (niche reference, all you need to know is that it's one of my bestest places to sit and smile) Hearing seagulls having a chat with each other but not nicking anyone's chips. Wearing shiny, new, silver shoes...

It's all about the small happy-making things, isn't it?

Grow Something (29th February 2020)

I seem to have ticked off another thing! I only have a teeny tiny bed by my steps and for the last few years I have just walked past its weedy messiness. Not anymore!

I cleared the weeds away, chucked on loads of compost (thanks Alex) and planted loads of bulbs and I've since been looking at the teeny tiny patch daily. And looky here, it's full of loveliness, with more to come! Hooray!

I also seem to have been growing ideas in an exciting way. Exciting and terrifying! I'm looking into training to become a celebrant. I'm currently deciding which course to take. And hopefully (fingers, toes, eyes and legs crossed!) I will be good to go in a few months.

So, if you need a celebratory celebrant, please bear me in mind!

In other news, thanks to Bar and Alison, a new element has been added to the daily trotting...dressage!

Out of county jaunts (16th March 2020)

I can add another two counties to the list...Kent and Essex! I've visited animals (Agatha and Rex, the gorgeous Maine Coone cats) I have tried two new tastes-ish...I had a couple of mouthfuls of Gewürztraminer and lunch at Five Guys (not at the same time I hasten to add!) One was more of a success than the other....

I trotted at Bluewater and on Southend pier...there may even have been a bit of skipping on the prom there too...in readiness for The Great Penzance Promenade Skip of 2020!

Oh yeh, I also saw friends from across the years! Garry has been my pal for about a million years and is very special (interpret that any way you will!) Mostly we talk nonsense and laugh a lot. He almost caused my early exit yesterday as he wanted me to attempt my cart wheeling challenge whilst on the pier. I felt it wasn't an ideal location given the gusty winds and my lack of co-ordination!

Visiting him and his fantastic wife, Elizabeth, is always a total joy. Especially now they have cats....

Now I am returning to Cornwall on the National Express coach (cue song) It takes about ninety-seven hours but only costs about 3 pence!

Apologies for any mistakes...it's quite jiggly on here!

33. Fix the door bell! (1st April 2020)

Well, I can tick that one off the list!

In these strange and unsettling times, I am trying to be kind to myself and not expect too much. I am also very grateful for my antidepressants. I'm not sure how well I'd be coping without them. It took me forever to ask for that particular type of help and I really wish I had done it sooner. Hindsight, eh? It's a wonderful thing! (is that a song title? Or have I imagined it? And do I now have an ear worm of an imaginary song in my head? Apologies, it's very late and I'm clearly wide awake!) Anyway, they have helped me feel like me again. And I realise that hadn't been the case for a very long time.

Luckily, I like my own company. Handy at the moment ph'sure! I am reading lots and lots, which is very lovely. In the morning, I try to sit out on my doorstep and read there for a bit whilst the sunshine catches that spot.

I have tons of things I know I could be doing...cleaning, sorting, being creative. But at the moment I am not able to do those things. And that is fine. There is time. For now, I need to let my head be.

I am aware I need to start moving more though...I may well be digging out the old Beverley Callard 'Shape Up and Dance' video soon! Now where are my leg warmers?

ps. I am aware that this post may be entirely nonsensical and apologise for my stream of consciousness. Thank you for bearing with me if you have reached this far! xx

2020...the year that went awry! (5th August 2020)

Well, this isn't what I had in mind!

But then...it's not just me, is it?!

So, what have I been doing 50 things wise? I've written (and received) a lot of mail. Although I did reach a sort of saturation point a while ago and I'm just gently easing myself back into it again.

I've grown something else. Much later than they should have gone in I popped in more bulbs and they've got a bit giddy and started bursting through the soil. Citing! And as I have such a poor memory box, I will get a smashing surprise when they flower!!

I planned to sew a frock but I've not been allowed near enough to an expert pal to get going. But, me being me, I have done trial subscriptions to two sewing magazines, bought various patterns and random bits of kit. I also now have my mummy's sewing box which must be a good omen. And I've purchased a sewing machine!!! Course I have. I have no idea if I can do it. And the one time I tried it, my straight lines really, really weren't! Ever the optimist...

I've found daily trotting rather tricksy on my own. I'm much more likely to do it with company it seems. Less so alone in my home during lockdown.

I've definitely not done lots of kissing nor had any naughty adventures. Sigh...

I've revisited some old favourites, film and book-wise but still have tons to go. That's a never-ending but lovely task.

I've done so much of the sorting of stuff. I can't say that it's finished because that would be a fib. And fibs are bad things!! However, I have made a sizeable dent in the mountains of stuff. It was very much done in small steps during lockdown but is pleasing. Hopefully, by the end of the year my home will be perfecto!! And I will be able to welcome visitors aplenty.

Which brings me to parties. And tea parties. And danceathons. And spending lots of time with friends and family. Hmmm, not so much. It'll be SO brilliant when we can do those things again!

My plans for my fast approaching 50th have obviously changed somewhat. No trip to Bath with family and chums. Not this year. Didn't you know that 51 is the new

50?! I shall still do a lovely something with my lovely blister. And see family. It'll be grand.

In other news, today would have been my 25th wedding anniversary. But bastard pancreatic cancer stole my Todd away. It was half my lifetime ago and I'm probably a pretty different person these days but I reckon I'd still marry him. He was a smasher. And loved a naughty adventure! Don't we all?

So, yeh, he didn't make it to 50…he stopped at 40. And, amongst a few other spectacular souls, I thought I'd do this here 50 things for 50 years mullarkey for him. And for me. Cos, I matter too apparently. Or so my counsellor tells me!!

Sorry, getting a bit dark there! It's late and it's been a difficult day. Normal service shall be resumed forthwith…

So, as soon as the prom in Penzance re-opens, I hope you will join me to skip along its length (ooer missus!)

ps I never expected that my 'performing lots' would entail rifling through my extensive costume collection to get filmed putting the bins out every week!!!

That came around quickly… (10th September 2020)

How is it September already?! And how can it possibly be less than two hours until the big 5 0? Surely that's still months away? I'm meant to have almost finished the 50 things for 50 years by now....

But then, 2020 happened, didn't it?

And this thing was meant to be about happy making stuff. It's not meant to be a competition with myself! I shall keep on plodding along achieving things as time passes. I've actually done quite a few of the things. No danceathon yet though…

But I will be spending my birthday in Bath as I'd hoped. Not with a bunch of friends and both my siblings…just with my bestest girl, my blister. And I shall be visiting animals too as we are going to the zoo (zoo zoo) (cue an earworm of a song…if you are of a certain age!)

At the beginning of the year, I was looking forward to 50 as it felt like a privilege to reach such a big number. Then over the last few weeks a certain fear took over. That fear that always seems to accompany a birthday with a zero at the end of it. What have I done with my life? Where am I going? That didn't go according to plan!!

But then, I received a hobby horse from my chums at work and realised, the trotting doesn't have to stop once I'm 50!!

And, just like that, I'm back to looking forward to this birthday...and all the others I hopefully get to have!

Happy Birthday Eve to me!!

My Birthday by Kate, aged 50 and 1/26th (25th September 2020)

So...this is 50

Not so very different from 49 really!

I ticked off a couple of the 50 things...visiting animals at Bristol Zoo and spending my 50th in Bath. I had a glorious time with my glorious blister. We laughed until we cried more than once. We chattered aplenty, ate wonderfully, shopped fulsomely and I trotted a whole heap.

It wasn't quite as planned. What is this year? But I had the best possible company. Sarah Jane Duggan. Nanash. Naughty. Sweetheart!

I also got to spend time with my daddy who laid on a lovely spread at his home in North Devon. And we were joined by my big bruv Kevin and his Katharine. The party continued to Dartmouth too…

So, yeh, 50 is OK so far! And there will be a Penzance party. Sometime.

Boy, will it be bloody marvellous!!

Kate has a scare (a fucking big one)

So, here's a thing, Kate is an excellent over-thinker. It is a skill she has honed over many years. However, she is equally adept at burying her head in the sand, sticking her fingers in her ears and going "la la la" to block out any unpleasant business. She is very aware of the workings of her body and 'what should be done' whilst being very capable of total self-sabotage in actually following those 'shoulds'. (She's never been a fan of 'shoulds')

In her head there is often a catastrophe occurring with every twinge or ache. Googling random symptoms late at night is a favourite hobby – her search history would tell many a tale! She thinks she's probably a bit like her mummy in that respect. Except her mummy didn't use Google.

But Kate tends to play most of these thoughts and catastrophes down most of the time – she doesn't want to be like her mummy with her loyalty card at the surgery, and it's mostly all in her (messy) head anyway.

Except when it isn't. And real symptoms start occurring. Being sick isn't normal is it really? But Kate can make it seem normal for ages...

"Probably something I ate"

"I ate too late"

"It was too rich"

"It disagreed with me"

"I was too greedy"

And the weight loss could be from her medication.

And the pains could just be bad luck.

And sleeping for 15 or 16 hours at a time? Well, she's been tired for such a long time – there was a lot of catching up to be done.

But in her head and with it being the 20-year anniversary, there's a voice screaming,

"IT MIGHT BE PANCREATIC CANCER...THAT WOULD BE SHITTY BAD LUCK, WOULDN'T IT?"

But if it's like it was back then, she doesn't think she'll sign up for chemo, cos it did fuck all and just stole loads of their precious time. No, she'll do it all on her terms. She'll fill what time she has left with lovely things. She'll go to London and see the shows she wants to see (Cabaret and Moulin Rouge mostly) and she'll see friends and maybe go somewhere sunny. And she'll organise everything so it's lovely and straightforward, her wishes will be clear. She'll even make a video for her funeral – trying to make her friends and family laugh, right until the very end. Not wanting them to suffer.

She'll die with humour and dignity. She'll just take painkillers and anti-sickness meds until she fades away.

But, before she goes, she wants to finish this bloody book and get it published. Even if no one ever reads it, she wants it to exist.

So, Kate mentions the sickness to her sister on the phone (playing it all down somewhat), who is rather concerned and tells her she should talk to the Doctor. But, as we know, Kate doesn't like 'shoulds' so she doesn't.

But when her sister sees Kate and remarks on her weight loss, the words pop out,

"Hmmm, it's not intentional"

And, later, Kate mentions it all to her nurse friend, who very swiftly springs into action. Drs appointments are made, blood tests conducted, 'samples' given and referrals made. And an appointment for a full CT scan arrives.

By then Kate is thinking,

"I haven't been sick for a few weeks, I mostly feel fine. I mean, I know I'm sleeping for Britain and I feel nauseous a lot of the time but, y'know, I haven't thrown up. So, I must be fine. I'm just wasting everybody's time. I'm making a fuss over nothing. It's going to be so embarrassing when it's not the worst thing it could be. I'm such a drama queen, wanting all the attention. Wasting valuable NHS resources. Maybe I should cancel the scan?"

She didn't cancel the scan.

The Day of the Scan

Well, I didn't sleep for Britain last night for sure. Hardly surprising really. I was watching back-to-back "Wild at Heart" in the early hours and then reading aplenty. Hey ho, the day has arrived. Karen has, very sweetly, insisted on coming with me to the scan as she knows I hate needles so much. And there's contrast to be popped into my system. Apparently, there is something exciting to expect – the sensation of wetting oneself is very common – it all sounds Jolly McJolly! Especially with my fear of that very same thing...

Sarah really wanted to come along too but I said it was silly cos I won't find out anything today. I'm working for a few hours, and she's got the weight of the world on her shoulders at the moment. I hope it was the right thing to do? I'm doing it for the bestest, most sensiblest reasons but I don't want her to feel rejected – not never. She is my bestest person after all.

So, my thoughts are veering between being riddled with cancer and having absolutely nothing the matter with me. And everything in between – it's quite exhausting.

I've not told many people about any of this – not wanting to worry anyone mostly. And it may well be nothing. Nothing at all!

After the Scan

Well, that was very odd indeed. Not the scan, that was fine. The introduction of the contrast dye,

"You'll feel a warm sensation when it goes in."

I thought it went in right from the get go so was feeling quite pleased that I hadn't felt the "warm sensation" as the tests started. Just the mechanical voice telling me when to hold my breath and when to breathe normally. (Why do we forget how to do this as soon as we are told to breathe normally? Or is that just me?) Just the noisy scanner and various other hospital-sounding noises. Then the voice of the radiographer,

"The dye is going in now. Warm sensation…"

Oh

Oh yes. All warm around my throat and my face and then 'oh my god, I've wet myself! I can't check cos my arms are up behind my head and I'm somewhat trapped'

I've been trying to keep my eyes closed through this experience in a Zen like way, but I'm pretty sure they snapped wide open at this point.

But, 'oh my god, that definitely feels like I've had a massive accident in my pants. And there's not a Tena Lady in sight. Oh, but it's abating a bit. But do my dungarees feel soggy? I'm really not sure'

Afterwards, when the lovely nurse comes out to detach me from the cannula and all the gubbins is over, I'm surreptitiously trying to check the gusset situation. We joke about the 'warm sensation', but I'm still trying to check and I'm SO relieved when I get up and the paper covering the bed is dry.

But, wow, that has to be the weirdest side effect going?

The Waiting

Trying to distract myself with lovely things. Work isn't a lovely thing but it does distract me too – even if I'm feeling considerably less patient than I ordinarily would be. Less inclined to indulge random concerns about crisp packaging or cable placement…

But, yes, still a lot of sleeping. Apart from when I can't because my heart is hammering in a petumpy tump fashion. I'm not worrying about when or how I'm sleeping – not whilst all this is going on. No sleep hygiene for me (to be honest, there rarely is)

And it seems that I am eating my feelings quite fulsomely. I have been for quite some time. The unexplained weight loss has ground to a halt. I feel sick if I don't eat and I feel sick if I do, so I'm eating. All. Of. The. Everything.

I'm also feeling responsible for other people's feelings. Quelle surprise! I hate that they are worrying about me. That's always been my role.

Still Waiting

My jiggly knee thing is back with a vengeance. I've always had it – I remember Annie putting a quietening hand on it in Crete when I was about 12 or 13, so it's not new. Mostly it stays quiet and doesn't bounce up and down like Billy Oh. However, at times of stress and worry, it takes on a life of its own. Currently, it's keeping itself very busy…jiggling.

I'm not sure if it counts as exercise but, if so, my right leg is getting a lot more of a workout than my left.

More Waiting

I started thinking about details for my funeral – like who would speak (I'd like Garry please) and got all upset. This was at Sarah's.

She spotted my blotchy, soggy face and a big cuddle ensued. I know she can't bear thinking about the possibility (if it were the other way round, neither could I)

I'm not sure how but we ended up talking about people wearing past costumes of mine. I mean, I do still own a lot of them! So here are some options...

The Sunshine from The Selfish Giant inspired by the story by Oscar Wilde (yellow mask and yellow and orange outfit)

One of the girls from Lechery Fair, inspired by Berholt Brecht and Kurt Weill (underwear and white face paint)

The Woman from The Same Old Story by Franca Rame and Dario Fo (leotard and tutu)

Madge from Female Transport by Steve Gooch (men's suit, bucket of cold water thrown over you, is optional)

Duchess of Berwick from Lady Windermere's Fan by Oscar Wilde (big, hired frocks, complete with hooped petticoats. Big hair)

Colin from Life of Riley by Alan Ayckbourn (tank top, cords, tweed jacket, brogues, Brylcreemed hair)

Mrs Cropley from The Vicar of Dibley by Richard Curtis (charity shop dress and crocheted jerkin, knitted hat, wrinkled tights, odd shoes)

Mrs Tinker from Vicar of Dibley Christmas by Richard Curtis (Christmas tree dress and penguin slippers)

Dullas D'Water (either a nautical 50s style frock and jaunty sailor's hat or a 20s style flappers dress with long beads and a feathered headband)

Frank Spencer (beret and a trench coat)

Margaret Thatcher (all blue skirt suit and blouse with pussycat bow, rosette)

Any character from The Rocky Horror Show. I may not have been in it but it has played a massive part in my life (whatever the hell you like!)

NB Stu is not allowed to wear a onesie, nor to look too cute. I'm sure he'd see the pulling potential of a funeral!

What If?

What if it is bad news?

Can I stay at home? My place is made of stairs and the bathroom is miles from my bedroom.

Would I get a keysafe?

Should I move in to the spare room?

I'd need to organise diet coke and food deliveries.

Will I be able to not pee myself whenever I am sick? Really hope so...I have a poor track record on that one!

Results

The scan was clear.

I thought I'd be skipping and jumping around with joy. But no. I have no idea how I feel. Not joyful for sure.

Am I disappointed? That'd be rather sick, wouldn't it? But I was so convinced that I was dying, that I could wind everything down, give no fucks, eat the everything, spend the non-existent money. Just do the good stuff, plan my final performance (aka a funeral) and wave bye bye.

I'd kind of omitted the pain and suffering of this option. And the fact that I'd be being a big bother.

But. But, it's not that. I am not exiting (pursued by bear or otherwise) in any imminent way it seems.

So, what is the matter? My symptoms have diminished certainly, but I'm not right.

Maybe that's why there's no skipping, nor trotting. Just a worry of a different sort – hopefully a less finite one though.

Waiting to see the Doctor

This time seems to be going on forever!

For those people I did tell, there's a mixture of continued worry and questions – or just a presumption that things have gone back to normal. I'm kind of treating it like that too really. Feeling like a bit of a fraud. And worrying that other people are worrying on my behalf.

I don't want to be a worry! Don't want to be a bother!

Mostly, I don't feel nearly as shitty as I did before. Still rather nauseous, still getting the gripey pains, blah blah blah!

It's Saturday, I'm in Cirencester with Garry and Elizabeth which is wonderful. I will be with them tomorrow too and then I'll see Gethin in Tewkesbury. Then on Monday I get to go to Ikea and Cribbs Causeway. Woop! I even have Café Rouge vouchers so that'll be a nice day too.

And then on Tuesday I'll see the Doctor who will probably just say it's,

The Menopause

The Diabetes

Being middle-aged

And to just get on with it.

Probably!

After Seeing The Doctor

Well, I'm none the wiser!

I seem to have flummoxed the Doctor. I thought that there would be further tests and stuff. But, no, the only suggestion was Gaviscon after meals. Which seemed a tad odd as heartburn wasn't upon the sizeable list of symptoms and I feel sick when I eat and when I don't.

But it's all calmed down a bit so she's happy for me to just contact them if needed.

To start with I was rather miffed about the appointment, as I'd been geared up for a raft of beastly investigations. As time has passed though, I'm much happier about it all. I still have stuff going on but, at this moment, there's nothing concerning and that's a relief after months of worrying.

I'm just a slightly slimmer version of me – unexpectedly!

January 1st 2023

I have a head full of sad.

It started in the run up to Todd's birthday. Usually, this anniversary isn't such a hard one. I think of him (well, that's a given, isn't it Kate?) but don't feel the need to do a 'thing'. More often than not I've worked (especially the 'duh duh duh' retail years) I might have done a facebook post but not much more. Although I still don't seem to be able to put up the Christmas decorations until after the 16th – an odd legacy that lives on, partially fuelled by my disorganised self!

So, December 16th 2022 loomed large in my head.

Y'see, Todd should have been 60 on that date. Fucking 60? Well, that's just ridiculous!

Beyond my incredulity lay so many thoughts though. So many questions. Would he have still been wearing (intentionally) odd socks? Would he still have driven round and round roundabouts, just because? Would he still be kayaking? Playing squash? Juggling? Getting stoned?

Would we still be living in Wantage? Would we have had a family? Would we have become proper grown-ups? Would we even have still been together?

I don't know.

I can't know – because Todd never made it past 40.

I've had a whole other life without him. He knows nothing of that and my friends down here in Cornwall know nothing of him. Apart from what I tell them and the photos that I share.

Todd is stuck in aspic (appropriate culinary based analogy there), in 2003, forever 40.

But that's not strictly true, is it? He's also in 1988, when I met him in his chef's whites, being shouty. And in 1995 when we got married on a very hot day. And in 2002 when we went on holiday to Corfu and talked about maybe, possibly starting a family. He is wrapped up and entangled in so many of my formative memories.

I'm just greedy, I would have liked 20 years more. Plus, the rest. I'm sure he'd have preferred that too!

Big birthdays do this, don't they? Make us think? Consider achievements or lack thereof? Make you wonder how you got to this point and how different it is to what you'd envisaged? And they make you look forward to what's – maybe, hopefully – to come.

But if you're having those thoughts on behalf of someone who wasn't lucky enough to reach another birthday with a zero at the end, then your head gets full of the what could have beens.

And that's why my heart and my head are sad.

I reckon he'd still be really fit, maybe doing ultra-marathons or somesuch nonsense.

He may well have been recognised for his services to local youngsters with his kayak training.

I cannot imagine he wouldn't still be enjoying a cheeky spliff.

And he'd definitely still be wearing odd socks.

These thoughts and imaginings helped me to get through his 60th. I took a day for me, for us, and I visited the Eden Project. I didn't go on the zipline – he would have. Nor did I cross the wobbly rope bridge – he'd have bounced across like Tigger. Nor did I climb to the highest part of the rainforest biome -he'd have been up like a shot. Instead, I had a bit of a cry (big bit) in the gardens where there were no other people to scare with my snotty, red face. And then I started to really take notice of my surroundings. I'd never seen as many robins as I did that day. The ground was especially frosty and the sunlight was angled blindingly low. I saw new pieces of thought-provoking art and noticed the absence of others. I was aware that the outside gardens were sleeping under their blanket of cold but knew that their blooms would return, all in good time.

I sat and watched Blue Infinity in the core building (if you've not seen it yet, google it as it's wonderful) and enjoyed the children's reactions to it. But then I stayed until it was just me and the "pup pup pup" sounds it makes as it expels its rings of vapour.

As that low sun disappeared, I entered the biomes which had been festive-ed right up (not with gingerbread houses and tinsel mind you) The Mediterranean biome had the biggest glitter ball that you ever did see suspended from the ceiling, with lights directed at it so that the whole space was turned into a wonderful disco garden – minus the Saturday Night Fever soundtrack, and the flares.

Then into the Rainforest biome, which blew my mind. Whoever did the sound and light installations in there deserves a big Hurrah and maybe a sherbet dibdab (high praise indeed)

For some reason I keep recalling 'son et lumiere' when I think back on the spectacle which is not so great. I mean, I know that's literally what it was, but my recollections of those seem to involve being on a school trip in the early 80s, outside a chateau on the River Loire in the dark (obviously Kate, not much point in the blazing sun). I recall rain and cold whilst 'enjoying' the 'spectacle' of a lit-up castle accompanied by a French soundtrack. I'm sure it was very interesting but I never understood any of it – sorry Miss Fogarty, you tried your best, but languages and me were sadly never great pals.

Whoops sorry, big digression there…

Anyhow, back to the rainforest. The overall feeling was magical and uplifting, which is just what I needed. In between the lit-up areas it was pretty damned dark so you couldn't really work out what plants and trees you were seeing, you just knew they were vast and luscious (sounds like a comedy duo I might be in!) I've been visiting Eden since it opened and it's such a world away from how it was in the beginning. Certainly, since Todd last visited in 2003 on my birthday.

The lights ranged from laser effects to banks of little suspended colour-changing frondy umbrellas and into soil-based wibbly, wobbly, slightly spinny white families of lights. It all chirped me right up.

And on the way home I got some KFC, as it was the nearest thing to a Miss Millie's I could get. (do they still exist in Weston-super-Mare?) And Todd was always partial to a bit of dirty chicken…

So, yeh, I coped with Todd's 60th – in my way.

But I know there are a lot more of these bittersweet (more bitter than sweet) memories to come this year as on October 6th 2023 it will be 20 years since Todd died.

Through the months ahead will be anniversaries and recollections of illness, diagnosis and treatments. I know it's going to be hard. I'm sentimental at the best of times. I can cry at an advert so my tear ducts don't stand a chance this year.

But, that's ok. It's natural to feel. To grieve. To welcome in all the emotions.

And that's why my head and my heart are full of sad.

2023

Dates I'm frightened of

16th December 2022 – Todd's 60th Birthday – Done

June -October 2023 -Diagnosis and Illness – Doing

October 6th 2023 – 20th Anniversary of Todd's Death – Waiting

Dates I'm Not Frightened of

February 13th – The Date we met for the first time

April 21st – Anniversary of our first date

May 1st – Anniversary of cherry popping!

August 5th – Our Wedding Anniversary

September 11th – My Birthday

The Lead Up to October 6th 2023

A lot of this year has gone by in a bit of a blur. I deliberately haven't been noting all of the dates I could have done. The dates when operations happened, when appointments were attended, when diagnoses were delivered.

I know I'm sentimental and I know I prefer to face the feelings head on, but on this, it seemed like a pretty self-destructive thing to do.

But I've been feeling increasingly jittery and unsettled as the year has progressed. And this week, the first week of October, I'm really on edge.

This isn't helped by Tom's increasing ill-health and being on red alert for what else will come his way. I'm permanently ready to pack a bag and head to North Devon because of another hospital admission or struggles at home.

But, underlying it all, is this very sad and unsettled feeling. It's like the lead up to a big birthday but without the promise of cake.

I'm evaluating my life it seems. Finding myself wanting somewhat. I don't seem to have created a legacy really...

No family created

No zingingly successful career

No financial stability.

But do I need to leave a legacy? Isn't being kind, funny, generous and thoughtful enough? Dunno, that depends on what my messy head tells me to believe on any particular day!

Alongside my unnecessary reckoning and its accompanying anxiety, there's a huge sadness. Of all that My Boy has missed out on. All the might have beens.

Sad and jittery. Not the greatest combo. Oh, and exhausted. And anxious. And overwhelmed. But better than not being here to experience any of it?

6th October 2023

Woke earlier than expected (needed a wee, as you do as a middle-aged personage)

Stayed awake. This is rare. Went back to bed – I'm not some sort of early morning convert! Had some (ahem) happy private time to start my day. Luckily some of those memories are still very vivid!

Crashing on – I pootled at home for a while. I had intended to visit the Gaia installation at Truro Cathedral as it opens today, plus visit the zoo. But I knew it would all be a bit of a rush and I didn't want that. I'll go another day.

So, I pootled. Changed my bedding from guinea pigs to foxes, popped on a guinea pig dress and went out. I readied the lounge for later with candles to be lit. And chose appropriate CDs for the car.

It was a beautiful sunny warm day. I got a sandwich and ate it at Longrock beach, looking at the sea and St Michael's Mount. Todd would have loved this view. He'd obviously have wanted to be on the water in his kayak. Or maybe he would have moved on to SUP-ing? Whatever, he'd have been doing it and I'd have been watching him!

The words from the chosen music were hitting me in the tear ducts. Kate Bush unexpectedly made me ugly cry. However, listening to Pink Floyd's Final Cut actually made me recall earlier times. The teenage years when I was full of angst and fury at the Conservative government (not much changes!)

All whilst I drove to Newquay Zoo. Todd would definitely have enjoyed it. I mooched around slowly – knowing what's around most of the corners. Loving the sounds of unseen creatures going about their business. And seen ones too – it'd be an odd zoo if all you experienced was unseen creatures.

I had a Cornetto with the sun on my back which was gorgeous! And I had a toddler touch my bottom (the unexpected perils of wearing a guinea pig dress) and wrote these words. On to the otters now.

I'll be back later…

Post October 6th

Clearly, I didn't write more later. I had an emotional but special evening. As there frequently is, Pink Floyd, candles and photos featured heavily. Also, a nice supper. And a lot of tears. I let it all out in a messy, snotty, red-eyed way but actually felt lighter and much more peaceful afterwards. The weight of the expectation of doom lifting I guess – or somesuch wanky phrase.

That was all good – until I felt the arrival of the The Nothing. A complete absence of feeling, motivation and joy. It's a frequent and unwanted visitor in my messy head. I know it. I do not welcome it. I want for it to bugger off.

So

So, how do I feel now that all the 20-year anniversaries have passed? A right old mixture of things, if I'm honest.

This was never going to be straightforward.

Mostly I feel lighter. I mean, this was a self-imposed period of reflection – I didn't need to impose extra pressure on my memory box.

But I've never taken the easy path with this grief mullarkey. I've faced all the crap head-on.

Was that right?

Was that wrong?

Who knows!

It's just what I did.

About pancreatic cancer

- Pancreatic cancer has the lowest survival of all the 20 common cancers. Less than seven per cent of people with pancreatic cancer will survive beyond 5 years in the UK. (Source: ONS)
- Five-year survival for pancreatic cancer has improved very little since the early 1970s.
- Around 10,500 people are diagnosed with pancreatic cancer per year in the UK. Around 8,924 people die every year of the disease in the UK.
- Surgery is the only treatment that can save lives, yet less than ten per cent of people with pancreatic cancer have it.
- Pancreatic cancer research has historically been underfunded. The disease attracts just 3 per cent of the UK cancer research budget. (Source: NCRI 2018/2019)

About Pancreatic Cancer UK:

- Pancreatic Cancer UK is taking on pancreatic cancer through research, support and campaigning to transform the future for people affected.
- We provide expert, personalised support and information via our Support Line (Freephone 0808 801 0707) and through a range of publications.

- We fund innovative research to find the breakthroughs that will change how we understand, diagnose and treat pancreatic cancer.
- We campaign for change; for better care, treatment and research, and for pancreatic cancer to have the recognition it needs.

Acknowledgments

Where do I start with this? Three More Days has been a very lengthy book to write. I may not have written every day since Todd died but this book has been on my mind often. As has Todd...you may have realised that already though!

A massive thank you must go to all the early readers of the book, who supported and encouraged me. And those fabulous women who agreed to proof read and advise and design for me. The ones who made it all real! To Kate, Jo, Jen, Hilary, Anna, Claire, Astra and Sarah, I bow down to your detail-seeking eyes and techy and creative knowledge.

I am lucky enough to have very supportive friends and family and I thank them wholeheartedly for listening and buoying me up.

A particular thank you must go to the Popsy Clothing community. If you don't know already, Popsy create the most fabulous dresses with the best designs going. And they have pockets! My first was a dress with books printed all over it and has been followed by others, most noticeably, guinea pigs! Anyway, they also have a Facebook community of the most wonderfully diverse, helpful and supportive members. Since I first asked about the credibility of publishing using KDP, these women, who I don't know have offered advice and support in spadefuls. They have read and responded to my lengthy posts and they are the most positive aspect of social media!

A huge word of appreciation for all the counsellors out there, not just the ones I used. You do remarkable work in helping us messy-headed folks.

I'd also like to extend massive appreciation to Kay from Rhubarb Tree who allowed me to use the image of her work on the cover of Three More Days. I wasn't lucky enough to buy this marvellous piece but I am grateful to be able to share the image. When I saw it, I just knew it was perfect.

And a final thank you must go to my sister, Sarah. She is Simply The Best!

About the Author

Kate is an experienced writer and performer, having run her own one-woman theatre company for 15 years, performed stand up, compered at various cabarets and performed many times at the wonderful Minack Theatre, in Cornwall. Her writing generally exists in the air, as it was mostly designed to be performed.

Along the way, she has also been a drama teacher, run the box office at her local theatre, she's been a barista, worked at events and in retail, run offices and been a P.A. It's been a varied work life for Kate – what is known as a portfolio career! And now she has completed a book.

A book that has been a long time in the writing.

Kate grew up in Somerset and these days she lives in West Cornwall…almost as far West as you can go without falling off! Along the way she has also lived in London and Oxfordshire. She shares her home with an excessive amount of pictures and ceramics.

Kate is a big fan of theatre, stand-up comedy, live music, going to the cinema for a cheeky matinee, reading, roast potatoes, guinea pigs, alpacas and wearing smile-inducing frocks.

Kate is not a fan of peas, sprouts or arrogant people.

Three More Days by Kate Morris has a page on Facebook and on Instagram, should you fancy following...

Printed in Great Britain
by Amazon